D1078073

MANAGING RISKS
IN
OUTDOOR ACTIVITIES

Cathye Haddock

Edited by Pippa Wisheart

Outdoor Safety

NEW ZEALAND MOUNTAIN SAFETY COUNCIL INC.

MEMBER ORGANISATIONS OF THE COUNCIL

Federated Mountain Clubs
NZ Alpine Club
NZ Ski Council
NZ Deerstalkers Association
NZ Shooting Federation
NZ Outdoor Instructors Association
Ministry of Defence
Department of Conservation
NZ Police
Ministry of Youth Affairs
NZ Tourist Industry Federation
ACC
NZ Sports Goods Association

COUNCIL'S MISSION STATEMENT

To promote responsible, safe and enjoyable use of the New Zealand bush and mountain environment.

Ⓑ796.5/HAD

Outdoor Safety

NEW ZEALAND MOUNTAIN SAFETY COUNCIL INC.

3rd Floor,
15-19 Tory St, Wellington
Tel: (04) 385-7162   Fax: (04) 385-7366

PREFACE

For over 25 years the NZ Mountain Safety Council has sought to promote responsible, safe and enjoyable use of the New Zealand bush and mountain environment. The outdoor environment itself, with its changing weather, and limitless opportunities for recreation, challenges us with a range of hazards depending on our activities and our abilities to look after ourselves in the outdoors.

The novice, with no experience or understanding of outdoor challenges, must depend on the skills and knowledge of an experienced person. As each of us gains experience, so we gain in self-reliance and the ability to manage the risks we encounter.

The effective management of risk is clearly outlined in this book through various stages, but is essentially based on a pro-active way of thinking. From the analysis of each activity, and the careful identification and assessment of each potential hazard and risk, through the process of eliminating, avoiding or reducing the risks to acceptable levels, to the disclosure of risks to our students, the processes of risk management are a powerful tool in the development of excellence in leadership. They follow, too, the current thrust of responsible safety management required by new legislation, and in particular the Health & Safety in Employment Act 1992.

In the writing of this book, Cathye Haddock has drawn widely from the knowledge and wisdom of many experienced outdoor teachers and leaders, both in New Zealand and overseas. This book breaks considerable new ground, and will become a valued addition to the range of outdoor texts published by the Council. The Council pays tribute to the work of all involved in this production.

Alan Trist
Executive Director

CONTENTS

LIST OF FIGURES

ACKNOWLEDGEMENTS

Thanks are expressed to the following people who have guided and assisted me in the preparation of this book:

Jill Dalton who has overseen the project from the seed of the first meeting to the fruition of publication, providing much encouragement, feedback and wisdom throughout.

Arthur Sutherland, Bert McConnell and Alan Trist, who along with Jill formed the core editing group. They challenged, debated, guided and advised me through various stages of the book's evolution. Their extensive experience, knowledge and background in risk management training was invaluable.

Liz Dickinson, Chris Knol, Gerald Rawson and Graham Egarr for their input into the early conceptual stages of the work.

Grant Davidson provided me with hospitality and a stimulating two days of discussion, debate and critical analysis of the material. I am indebted to his incredible depth of knowledge and academic understanding of the topic. For me, this was a great anchor point for the academic integrity of the book.

Special thanks to Henry Sunderland for his excellent drawings. His injections of humour and fun cleverly lighten some of this material.

A huge thanks to the many authors and outdoor leaders whose work is quoted in this book. Their experiences and painstaking study and research in the many aspects of risk management over the years, have provided a rich tapestry from which we can all learn. I also acknowledge the current and future workers in this field for their contributions to this 'never ending' topic.

To my partner Peter Simpson for his unending patience and support throughout the seemingly 'never ending' project.

To Professor Timoti S. Karetu, Commissioner Te Taura Whiri i te Reo Maori, for translating the Definitions of Terms into the Maori language.

Finally to Pippa Wisheart for editing the final draft. Her sensitivity, skill and professionalism were impressive!

Cathye Haddock

INTRODUCTION

RISK is an integral part of taking groups into an outdoor setting whether rural, urban or wilderness. Outdoor activities are playing an increasing role in education, recreation and youth programmes. Research and experience show that although such activities can help learning and contribute significantly to personal growth, they also have potential, when poorly led, to have negative outcomes. Poor leading often stems from a lack of awareness.

This manual provides an in-depth look at the nature and structure of risk, suggests ways it can be modified to acceptable levels in outdoor activities and offers guidance on what to do if a crisis does occur.

It examines some working tools for identifying, reducing and managing RISK factors in outdoor activities, in terms of the

PEOPLE,
RESOURCES, EQUIPMENT and
ENVIRONMENT involved.

The RISK MANAGEMENT planning procedures and SOUND PROFESSIONAL PRACTICE advocated in this manual, are intended for all people taking on responsibility for others in the outdoors. It will be of particular value to teachers, outdoor instructors and assistant instructors, youth group leaders, club people and community recreation workers.

CHAPTER 1

RISKY BUSINESS—
THRILLS, CHILLS and SPILLS
Why manage risk in outdoor activities?

GENERAL

It is widely accepted that adventure-based outdoor educational programmes offering **risk** are a medium for personal growth and development and team building. They are a popular component of many school, recreation and community programmes. Society however, does expect outdoor leaders to keep **risks** at 'acceptable levels'.

The concept of risk management is not a new idea. The Chinese express the concept of risk and its relationship to the development and education of the individual with the term 'wei-jan'. Translated it means danger and opportunity; the very essence of why we place people into risky situations, whether the danger is real or imaginary. Without the danger the opportunity evaporates![1] Indeed our own country's heritage was founded on this concept.

> Kupe, leader of the legendary great migration to Aotearoa, led his people through many dangers in search of the new land. The sheer uncertainty of the voyage encapsulated the risks they took. In essence, they risked their lives on this journey. But their successful discovery of Aotearoa and all the new opportunities this provided, turned their risk into reward. (The dangers into opportunities).

Latter day adventurers still want a sense of adventure and challenge in outdoor activities, but have no intention of being injured. In other words, most people want the appearance but not the essence of risk so participants too expect outdoor leaders and providers to protect them from any real harm.

1

Apart from preventing real risk to the lives or well-being of people, there are many kinds of risks for the outdoor leader to be aware of: **psychological, emotional, physical, cultural, social, gender and spiritual**. If a learner is not willing or able to repeat an act, it is worth considering whether it was an unsafe act for them.

There are obvious moral reasons for leaders to manage risks in outdoor activities but there are also some very real legal reasons for doing so.

The law requires outdoor leaders to provide a high **standard of care**, which is in keeping with **sound common practice**. In the case of minors, this **care** should compare to that of a careful and prudent parent (*in loco parentis*). In the case of adults, the nature of care would differ from that owed minors, but the standard would not. (Appendix A, see page 89, details the moral, legal and professional responsibilities of outdoor educators and administrators).

THE OUTDOOR GAMBLE

The following analogy could be likened to what could happen when you take a group outdoors. Imagine a slot machine, a one armed bandit bolted to a tree.

Fig. 1: The Outdoor Gamble

Imagine too that every time you take a group into the outdoors you are putting a coin into the slot and pulling the handle down. Each time a risk factor is overlooked or ignored, up pops a **lemon** in one of the windows. As more risk factors are overlooked, more lemons are lined up. The process continues until you either arrive at the end of the activity or you rack up enough lemons to hit the JACKPOT . . . DISASTER![2] Competent, experienced leaders are always on the look out for lemons which they deal with before they can cause accidents. For example:

A youth leader preparing their group for an overnight tramp checks everyones' gear and find two people without adequate parkas and one without any woollen or pile clothing (3 lemons). The leader fits the students with the clothing they need from a box of spare gear. Checking the medical list the leader finds there are two asthmatics in the group and one person allergic to bee and wasp stings. The leader explains to the latter that if they travel at the front of the party their chances of being stung are reduced significantly.

In the first aid kit are a spare inhaler and an ana-kit to treat severe allergic reactions to stings. If the leader continues to be as conscientious as this throughout the trip, most disasters will be avoided. If the lemons are overlooked by the leader circumstances could combine and the JACKPOT could be struck.

(See Chapter 6 for a closer look at lemons and what we can learn from them).

It can be argued that the outdoors is not inherently dangerous. The environment itself is neutral. It is only when people go into the outdoors that problems can occur.

This manual looks at ways of recognising risks in the outdoors, assessing them and if necessary managing them to ensure high quality experiences are achieved for the learners or participants.

First of all what does research say . . . .

THE TIP OF THE ICEBERG

One study[3] identified a 1:10:30:600 relationship between serious and minor events.

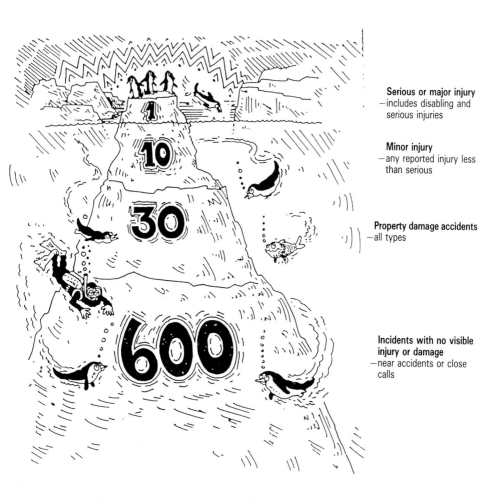

Serious or major injury
—includes disabling and
serious injuries

Minor injury
—any reported injury less
than serious

Property damage accidents
—all types

**Incidents with no visible
injury or damage**
—near accidents or close
calls

Fig. 2:   Accident Ratio Study[4] (Bird and Germaine 1987)

This industrial study concluded that many incidents have similar causes to accidents, so it would be unwise to concentrate solely on the few serious or disabling injuries which happen. If you did, you would only be seeing the TIP OF THE ICEBERG. Investigating 600 stubbed toes is not going to prevent a river drowning, however incidents with high potential for harm need to be investigated as thoroughly as accidents.

The following is a good example of similar incidents which needed further investigation although no one was seriously injured.

Over a period of six months in an outdoor programme, four incidents were recorded where a stove slipped off a bench while students were cooking. In each case a billy was being stirred on top of the stove. The stove shot out from under the billy, falling to the floor and spreading burning meths everywhere. No-one was physically hurt although students got a real fright. There was no damage to property either.

Investigations found these common factors contributed to the incidents:

— the stainless steel benches in the huts provided a slippery surface for the legs of the stove
— students stirring the contents of a large billy while it was perched on the top of the stove
— the billies being used were old and had very uneven bottoms.

To prevent similar accidents in the future the following changes were made:

• New billies were purchased to replace old battered ones.
• Students were instructed to carry billies inside packs to reduce damage.
• Billy grips were provided with each billy.
• Students were instructed to remove the billy from the stove when stirring.

Research[5] also confirms that not only do many incidents and accidents have similar causes, but the seriousness of the incident is purely a matter of chance!

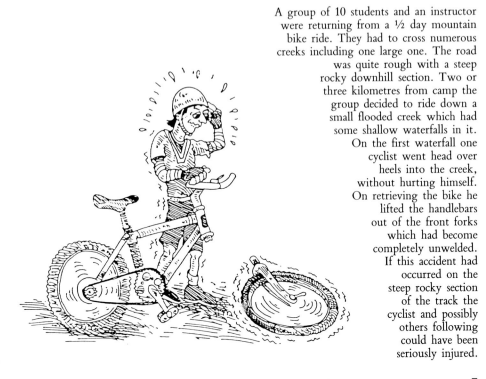

A group of 10 students and an instructor were returning from a ½ day mountain bike ride. They had to cross numerous creeks including one large one. The road was quite rough with a steep rocky downhill section. Two or three kilometres from camp the group decided to ride down a small flooded creek which had some shallow waterfalls in it. On the first waterfall one cyclist went head over heels into the creek, without hurting himself. On retrieving the bike he lifted the handlebars out of the front forks which had become completely unwelded. If this accident had occurred on the steep rocky section of the track the cyclist and possibly others following could have been seriously injured.

5

Although no one was harmed in this accident it needed thorough investigation. The investigation found the bike was old and ill-maintained and had been given voluntarily for use on the programme. The organisation decided to hire well-maintained bikes for future programmes.

This risk management manual will look mainly below the waterline at the submerged iceberg. It is here where we will find the greatest opportunities for learning, forward planning and preventive action, so we can make the changes necessary to prevent the TIP OF THE ICEBERG coming into sight (that is, a serious accident happening).

Accordingly, this text is illustrated extensively with incidents rather than serious accidents. All incidents used are actual New Zealand examples however names and locations have been altered to preserve anonymity!

CAUSES OF ACCIDENTS

What does the research show here? The majority of accidents and incidents are usually the result of an unfortunate combination of any of the following:

— an unobserved or underestimated unsafe condition
— an unsafe act, on the part of the student or
— an error of judgement on the part of the instructor.

Examples are given below.

Principal causes of major accidents in adventure programmes		
Unsafe conditions	Unsafe acts	Errors of judgement due to:
Swift water	Poor position	New or unexpected situation
Loose rock	Unauthorised procedure	Desire to please others
Inadequate area security	Unsafe speed	Misperception
Unexpected water/ Improper clothing	Inadequate water/ Nutrient intake	Fatigue/ Distraction

(Dan Meyer 1979)[6]

Fig. 3: Principal causes of major accidents in adventure programmes

Industrial research[7] shows almost identical results.

Behind the immediate causes listed here, it has been shown that fundamental factors exist at the management level of the programme. These will be discussed in detail in Chapter 6.

ACCIDENT PREVENTION

'An analysis of fatal accidents from 1945-1961 done by the Federated Mountain Clubs (Bulletin 12) found equal numbers of experienced and inexperienced people among the victims. Furthermore, 92% of these accidents were considered **avoidable**. Only 8% were beyond the control of the recreationist. This analysis and a subsequent one published in 1967 (Bulletin 28) with similar findings strongly support the view that physical events (such as lightning) are much less important than human actions'.[8]

Some people would argue that **all** accidents are preventable with enough preventative planning and information gathering e.g. should the group be out in the lightning in the first place? There are obvious limits to how far a leader can go in their planning, while still meeting the requirements of 'Duty of Care owed to students'.

All research seems to point to the common sense value of **planning** in order to reduce the chance of having accidents. When planning to reduce accidents, it is helpful to consider four major factors in the total picture:

—PEOPLE   —RESOURCES and EQUIPMENT

—ENVIRONMENT   —ACTIVITY

By looking closely at these areas, risks can be identified and a safety or risk management plan put into place.

The following chapters set out the basic principles of risk management and provide some effective tools for **planning** to reduce accidents.

CHAPTER 2

DEFINITIONS OF TERMS
Are we speaking the same language?

To establish a common language, definitions of terms used frequently in this manual are set out on the following pages.

ADVENTURE

> An experience where the outcome is **uncertain** because key information may be missing, vague or unknown.

Yet to the adventurer, it must appear possible to influence the circumstances in a manner which provides hope of resolving the uncertainty.

An adventure is much like **leisure:**
- a state of mind
- freely chosen
- intrinsically motivating
- may lead to a peak experience.

The adventure experience is individually specific due to competence, situationally specific because of risk, and chronologically specific in time.

An adventure for one person, in a certain place and at a particular time, may not be an adventure given a different person . . . place . . . or time.[1]

PEAK EXPERIENCE

> The pleasurable feeling someone feels when they are performing to their physical and sensory potential.

Researchers have found that this feeling can be attained during many activities, e.g. surgery, rockclimbing, chess, dancing. People who enjoy what they are doing, and are competent at it experience a euphoric state. They concentrate their attention on the task, forget personal problems, lose their sense of time and of themselves, feel competent and in control, and have a sense of harmony and union with their surroundings. Risk (uncertainty) and danger are critical to the peak experience, as they heighten concentration.[2]

Peak experiences are common during well run outdoor adventure activities, and because they are remembered as important and desirable, adventurers seek to repeat them.

CHALLENGE

> The interplay of risk and competence.

For an adventure experience to be challenging it must include an element of competence effected in an effort to resolve the uncertainty.

Poker, video-games, outdoor pursuits are examples of activities which involve challenge.[3]

CHANCE

> A random event.

An adventure experience which is not influenced by the skill of the participants relies for outcome on chance.

Lotto, scratch poker, crossing serac fields at any time of day, are examples of activities which involve chance.[4]

COMPETENCE

> The ability of an individual to deal effectively with the demands placed on them by the surrounding environment

In any adventure situation this ability relates directly to skill, knowledge, attitude, behaviour, confidence, and experience aimed at solving problems and avoiding the negative consequences of risk.[5]

Competence is the ability to resolve the uncertainty.

RISK

> The potential to lose something of value. The loss may be physical, mental, social or financial. The presence of risk creates uncertainty.[6]

It appears therefore that **risk** relates to **consequences** and has a measure of **probability or uncertainty** associated with it. The motivation for risking is to gain something of value. That something in the outdoors is the challenge of an adventure.

DANGER

> Risks arise from dangers.
> Dangers come in two forms:
>
> | PERILS | HAZARDS |
> |---|---|
> | The source of the loss. | Conditions which increase the likelihood of the loss. |
> | For example: | For example: |
> | • cut rope | • sharp edge |
> | • lightning bolt | • summit of mountain in storm |
> | • falling rock. | • badly positioned. students[7] |

11

ACCIDENT

> An undesired event which results in harm to people, damage to property or loss to process.[8]

There are four important aspects to this definition.

- It doesn't limit human results to 'injury', but says 'harm to people'. This could involve injury or illness (mental or physical).
- It does not confuse 'injury' with accident. They are not the same. Injuries and illnesses result from accidents but not all accidents result in injury or illness. The severity of the injury itself is often a matter of chance.
- If the event results in property damage or process loss alone, and no injury, it is still an accident.
- Loss to process is an interruption or disruption to routine or the programme.

    Often accidents result in harm to people, property and process.

INCIDENT

> An undesired event which, under slightly different circumstances, could have resulted in harm to people damage to property or loss to process.
>
> An undesired event which could or does result in a loss.[9]

This term as related to safety, is usually referred to as the 'near accident' or the 'near miss'. William G. Johnson, author of a widely acclaimed book on safety, states that the incident is similar to an accident, but without injury or damage. He goes on to state that incidents are enormously important to safety. An incident with high potential for harm should be investigated as thoroughly as an accident, in order to learn how to prevent a similar occurrence in the future.

SAFETY

> Control of accidental loss.[10]
>
> (Bird and Germain 1987)

Control is the act of managing, so safety is actually managing the potential for loss (risk). Its major goals are to manage and minimise risk and eliminate accidents i.e. to eliminate the potential for harm to people, damage to property or loss to process.

STANDARDS

> Specification by which the qualities required of something may be tested.[11]

Before risk can be controlled, there must be standards of safety to aim for. In the outdoor setting, these are developed by the controlling authority, the people involved in the activity or the appropriate national body. For example:

ACTIVITY	BODY RESPONSIBLE FOR STANDARDS
Kayaking	NZ Canoeing Association
Education Outside the Classroom	Boards of Trustees
An adventure game on the beach	The people playing it and perhaps the leader

RISK MANAGEMENT

> The process of reducing potential loss to an acceptable level.[12]

How much risk is acceptable?

How do we justify this acceptable level of risk to others?

As independent adventurers we are free to accept the risks and rewards of adventure for ourselves. As outdoor educators, using adventure as a tool to achieve educational objectives, we are responsible for our charges and their rights under the law. We may have professional motives, sharing the benefits of an adventure experience with others. Society, however, has greater concerns. It has less sympathy for us if things go wrong, labelling such adventures as foolhardy and dangerous. To assist outdoor educators to justify putting people at risk, Baillie[13] proposes the model of 'Normal Life Risk'.

This model was based on comparing accident data from everyday normal life activities with that of outdoor adventure-based programmes. One study[14] found that Outward Bound courses had a lower ratio of disabling injuries than either automobile driving or college football. The other[15] reported fewer deaths due to outdoor adventures than due to automobile accidents.

This comparison showed that **adventure experiences are no more risky than everyday living**.

13

It seems unrealistic then to eliminate all fatalities and disabling injuries from adventure-based programmes. **It appears both practical and defendable however, to reduce fatality and disabling injury rates to the level associated with the process of everyday living.**

If outdoor educators wish to win the trust of society and establish credibility as a profession, clear responsible risk management procedures supported by stringent accident data collection, must be set up and followed.[16]

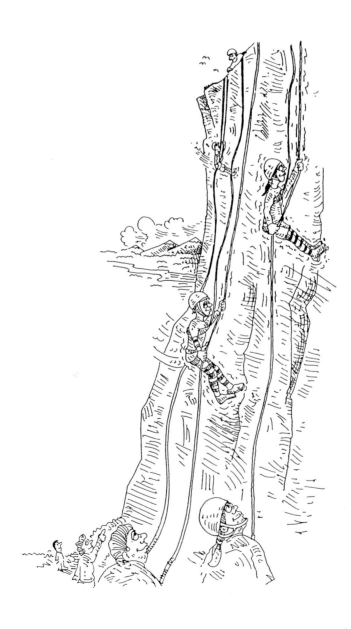

DEFINITIONS OF TERMS IN TE REO MAORI

TŪWHETA — Adventure
He mātangatanga kāore i te mōhiotia he aha tōna otinga atu nā te mea kei te hapa ētahi pārongo kāore rānei i te mārama, kāore rānei i te mōhiotia.

PANEKIRETANGA — Peak Experience
Ko te tino tau o te mauri nā te mōhio o te tangata kua taea e ia tā tōna tinana i tōiri ai.

WHAKAHORO — Challenge
Ko te pā atu o te whatitata ki te āheinga o te tangata.

E whakahoro ai te mātangatanga tūwheta me mātua uru atu he wāhanga āheinga e hāngai ana kia kitea ai me pēhea taua warawara e whakakoretia atu ai.

HEIPŪTANGA — Chance
He pāpono nā te wā.

He mātangatanga tūwheta kāore i te riro noa mā te pūkenga o te tangata engari kei te waiho kē mā te wā.

ĀHEINGA — Competence
Ko te āhei o te tangata ki te whakautu i ngā whakahau mai i a ia a te taiao e karapoti ana i a ia.

Ahakoa he aha te tūwheta, ko tēnei āheinga e hāngai pū atu ana ki te pūkengatanga, ki te mātauranga, ki te whaiarotanga, ki te whanonga, ki te anitūnga me te mātangatanga e rite ana hei hīrau raru, hei karo anō hoki i ngā āhuatanga kino o te whatitata.

WHATITATA — Risk
Ko te torohū e ngaro ai tētahi āhuatanga e matoa nuitia ana ahakoa ā-tinana, ā-hinengaro, ā-tangata, ā-pūtea rānei. Nā whatitata ko warawara!

TĀTĀTUMA — Danger
Nā te tātātuma ko te whatitata.

E rua ngā āhuatanga o te tātātuma: ko te *pūmate*, arā, ko te pūnga mai o te mate me te *matepā*, arā, ko ngā āhuatanga e tino pā ai te mate.

15

Hauata — Accident

He pāpono kāore i te hiahiatia, ā, ko tōna otinga atu ko te whara o te tangata, ko te tūkinotia o ngā rawa me te korenga i okea o ngā taumata.

Maiki — Incident

He pāpono kāore i te hiahiatia, ā, mena i rerekē noa atu kua whara kē ko te tangata, kua tūkino kētia ko ngā rawa, kua kore i ekea ngā taumata.

He pāpono kāore i te hiahiatia, ko tōna otinga atu rānei ko te pā o te mate.

Pareora — Safety

Ko te āhei ki te ārai i ngā hauata poka noa.

Paerewa — Standards

Ko ngā whakaritenga e taea ai te whakamātau ngā pai, ngā kino rānei o tētahi mea.

Ārai Whatitata — Risk Management

Ko te āhei ki te whakaiti i te mate torohū ki tōna pae e whakaaetia ai.[17] [18]

16

CHAPTER 3

PRINCIPLES OF RISK MANAGEMENT
Why risk in the first place?

INTRODUCTION

If RISK is defined as the potential to lose something of value, then the motivation for risking must be to gain something of value. Involvement in risk activities can provide many positive outcomes for people. Many seek risk to fulfil their desire for memorable, joyful experiences and feelings. Outdoor adventure activities hold a strong attraction because they provide opportunities for people to experience the uncertainty associated with risk and adventure, which can lead to peak experiences. Such experiences are extremely positive and self-validating. They are important experiences which are learned from again and again so people seek to repeat them. For example :

> The student who had never tested her endurance and stamina before a tramp, now realises that if she can survive the long steep climb up a mountain in foul weather, she can survive anything! Unconsciously, she will have absorbed that she has a strength and determination she never knew she had. Consciously, she decides to take up tramping.

People have described their 'peak experiences' as 'magic', 'everything just jelled', 'flowed', 'they just came together', because they are such powerful, even joyful times.

Many things of value can be gained by having adventure experiences:

- increased self esteem
- increased self confidence
- the exhilaration of overcoming or facing challenges
- a sense of achievement and wellbeing.

These are all accepted educational objectives for outdoor programmes and RISK can be used as an effective tool to achieve them.

RISK IDENTIFICATION

The **risks** associated with any activity must first be **identified** before they can be dealt with. For example:

> An early childhood teacher planning to take a group of pre-schoolers to the fire station may identify the following possible risks:
> - Injury around equipment/engines.
> - Psychological damage—fear of fire engines.
> - Process of learning impaired.

Once the risks inherent in the activity have been identified, the next step is to identify the likely **causal factors** which would result in those risks being realised. Causal factors are in fact dangers.

Causal factors may be grouped under three main headings for ease of identification— people, equipment and environment.

At the planning stage of the trip to the fire station, the following causal factors could be identified:

People (children, 4 yr olds)
- Unsuitable helpers.
- Medical problems of children.
- Child falling from engine.
- A child getting lost.

Equipment/Resources
- Car breaking down or being separated from convoy.
- Fire engines could be called out.
- Fire engines big compared to size of children.

Environment
- Stimulating environment—could distract attention.
- Possible danger areas—exits, entrances.
- Siren noise could panic children.
- Confined space.

It is important to accurately identify the risks and dangers associated with an activity so they can be managed to an acceptable level.

> Imagine that the fire alarm went off during the pre-school group's visit to the fire station, and in the confusion a child fell off the engine and broke a wrist.

Figure 4 shows that an accident often has a variety of causal factors (lemons) which may combine to cause an accident. It also shows how important it is to be able to **identify** causal factors, so you can plan to **reduce** them.

This simplified causal sequence will be discussed in more detail in **Chapter 6**.

This accident can be broken down simply into the following stages:

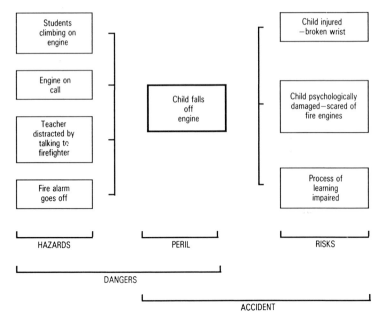

Fig. 4: Fire station accident—model showing a simplified causal sequence
(Adapted from Kates, Hohenemser & Kasperson, 1985)

19

TYPES OF RISK

There are three possible values for risk:

Absolute Risk

The uppermost limit of the risk inherent in a situation (no safety controls present).

Real Risk

The amount of risk which actually exists at a given moment in time (absolute risk adjusted by safety controls).

Perceived Risk

Any individual's subjective assessment of the real risk present at any time.

Note:

- The **absolute risk** for any activity at a certain point in time is constant.
- The **real risk** for any activity is also constant but can't be determined.
- The **perceived risk** for any activity differs from person to person and may not be related to either the real risk or absolute risk.[1]

To illustrate let's look at a caving trip. The absolute risk associated might be the worst possible scenario of someone getting completely stuck in a squeeze. The perceived risk might be concern that some people will have difficulty in one of the squeezes, and the real risk might be that no-one gets stuck or has difficulty at all.

Absolute values of risk are of lesser importance in an adventure. The perceived and real values play more important roles.

When identifying risks you must be aware of the differences between real and perceived risk. These can vary greatly from person to person and it becomes a complex area. To simplify, everyone has their own idea of the risk involved. What appears to be risky to one person may not be to another. The risk inherent in or associated with, a particular activity is **real risk**. How a person sees it in their own mind is **perceived risk**.

People may be influenced by any one or more of such factors as:

- confidence level
- equipment (familiarity)
- venue
- leader
- experience level
- mood
- degree of tiredness
- psychological makeup
- awareness of own limitations
- knowledge of the situation
- fear of the unknown.

All activities have a level of real risk with different people having different perceptions of what this level is (perceived risk). These risks, if identified, can often be modified to acceptable levels.

The risks in each of the following photographs are quite different. Can you identify them? To what extent have risks been 'managed' in each photograph? Which is the safer activity?

Fig. 5(a) Snow sliding

Fig. 5(b) Crevasse field

The instructor's role is to put into place effective strategies which will modify both types of risk to acceptable levels, using one or a combination of the risk reduction strategies outlined later in this chapter. Problems can arise when there is a mismatch between real and perceived risks.

The following model illustrates matching and mismatching:

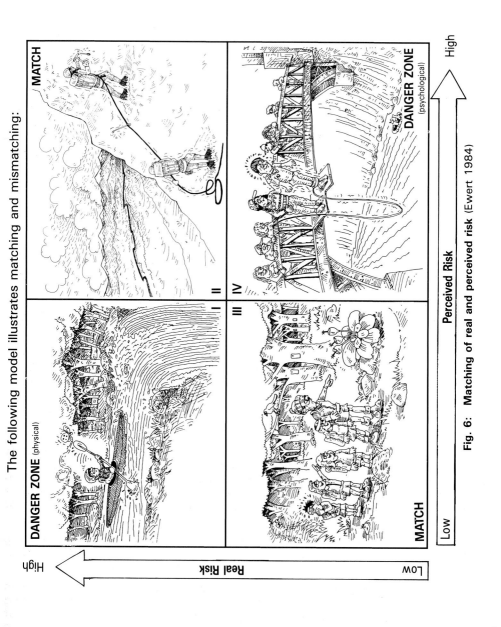

Fig. 6: Matching of real and perceived risk (Ewert 1984)

22

Perceived risk will not necessarily relate to real risk but may contribute to it in some situations. The following is an outline of the consequences of matching and mismatching:

Areas

I	The real risk is high but the perceived risk is low. Participants in the activity may not recognise the real risk present. For example, kayaking down an unknown river, oblivious to the waterfall at the bottom of the next rapids.

II & **III**	Where real and perceived risk (whether high or low) match one another there is no problem as the person is aware of the actual situation and can deal with it accordingly.

IV	High perceived risk in a low real risk situation. For example with bungy jumping a participant may be so frightened that although they jump and come to no harm, they have nightmares for weeks afterwards, suffering ongoing psychological damage.

A high level of perceived risk is often manifested in fear or anxiety in an individual. From an outdoor educator's perspective, it is important to judge how much fear is present and when it occurs in order to manage the activity effectively to avoid psychological damage and ensure: HIGH QUALITY EXPERIENCES for learners.

Conversely, a low level of perceived risk in a high real risk situation can manifest itself in boredom and carelessness. This could lead to physical danger to the individual. The instructor in this case needs to manage the activity in a way which brings the person's perception of the risk closer to reality. In some situations the instructor can be the one at risk of boredom and carelessness. He or she must be aware of this danger and try to avoid it.

For those who are new to an activity, there are few, if any situations where exposing them to high levels of real risk is the only way to achieve educational objectives. Instructors should always avoid putting novices into this type of situation.

Many outdoor programmes deliberately include activities where participants perceive an element or risk. When a person overcomes a difficult challenge, using skills which have been learned in a progressive manner and with the support of a group, a powerful success experience can be generated (peak experience). This can occur when appropriate levels of risk are used and combined with well-developed educational objectives to achieve high quality experiences for the learner.

ASSESSMENT OF RISK

When the risks associated with an activity have been identified the next step is to assess the amount of risk present.

Factors involved are again: people, equipment, environment.

If these three factors are kept separate, there can be no risk.

The greatest potential for risk is when the three factors combine during an activity.

Fig. 7: Interrelation of people, equipment, environment

Someone will need to take responsibility for the actual assessment of risk present during the activity (usually the leader or person responsible for organising the activity). This person must use their **judgement** to make a sound assessment of the risks, weighing all the **factors**. Judgement involves experience, skill, and knowledge of the activity, people, environment and equipment involved.

The leader's assessment involves asking the question:

How much risk is acceptable?—while considering **the value of risk activities**.

Very safe—but does this detract from the value of the activity? (Without the risk the opportunity evaporates!).

Too much risk.

Somewhere in between is the right balance.(A practical and defendable level of risk).

Fig. 8: Assessment of risk levels

The following is a risk versus safety meter which shows the types of risk under consideration by the instructor.

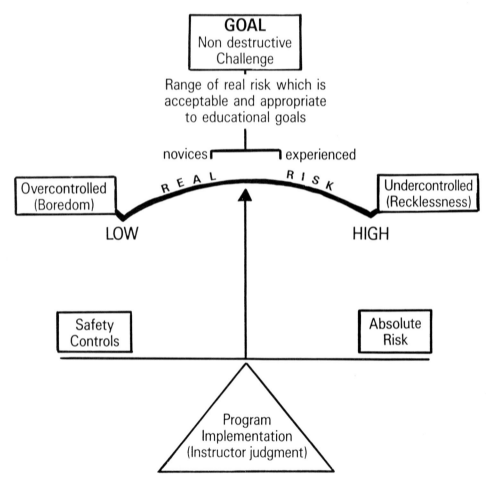

Fig. 9: **Risk versus safety meter** (Davidson 1992)

The leader/s can continue with the activity if the outcome of the assessment is that the risk level is acceptable. Too much risk, however, is unacceptable and the leader/s must consider options at this point, using their judgement.

Here is how to consider the options:

THE DECISION-MAKING PROCESS

When evaluating risk potential in outdoor activities, and making decisions accordingly the four windows matrix (fig. 10) may prove useful. This matrix weighs up the severity of the condition with the likely occurrence of an incident/accident and offers four standard decisions which may be applied: reduction, avoidance, transference, retaining of the risk.

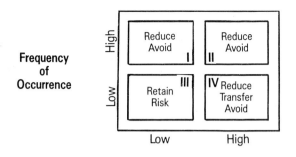

Frequency of Occurrence

Severity of Condition

Fig. 10: **Four windows matrix** (Adapted by Davidson 1992 from Ewert 1984)

Retain risk — Keep it because you have assessed that the frequency and severity are low.

Reduce risk — Use strategies to do this.

Avoid risk — Frequency or severity are at an unacceptable level despite efforts to manage them in all possible ways.

Transfer risk — Either to a more skilled leader **or** give the participants the information to make the choice and take the responsibility themselves.

The aim of this process is to try to put yourself in a situation where the risks to be taken are at an acceptable level. In other words, you are trying to get yourself into box III, operating in the low frequency, low severity realm.

	Area	Example	Recommended Action/Decision
I	High Frequency Low Severity	Blisters	•**Reduce risk** by taping feet up. •**Avoid risk** by not tramping or not using boots.
II	High Frequency High Severity	Diving in water hole with snags	•**Reduce risk** by removing snags. •**Avoid risk** by banning diving.
III	Low Frequency Low Severity	Sprained ankle on tramping trip	•Retain risk potential, Go on trip anyway.
IV	Low Frequency High Severity	Alpine Snowcraft Course in winter. No qualified instructors on staff.	••**Reduce risk** by choosing safe terrain which staff can handle. •**Transfer risk** by getting NZMSC or other competent instructors in. •**Avoid risk** by cancelling course.

Fig. 11: **Decision-making options**

26

RISK REDUCTION STRATEGIES

There are many ways of modifying risk levels before and during activities. If, as a leader, you decide there is too much risk involved in the activity you have planned, consider one or a combination of the following strategies to **reduce** the risks.

THE USE OF RULES POLICIES AND GUIDELINES

Human based hazards   Environment based hazards

Fig. 12: **Use of rules to modify risk levels** (Hale, 1984)

For example: On a kayaking trip, people are at risk in a river environment. Given good boats and lifejackets, adequate skills for the river and normal river flow, the risks are reduced significantly on the trip. However accident potential can escalate when even one wild card is thrown in, e.g. bad weather during the trip, unknown snags from a recent flood, several students with flu, an instructor who has not paddled for years. One way of eliminating accident potential is to introduce **rules** to keep people out of certain situations. The following policies could be effective in reducing some of the risks associated with the river trip above.

- Only instructors with **current** logged river experience or an NZOIA Kayak 1 Qualification can instruct students on river trips.

- River trips must be postponed if bad weather is forecast and more than 10mm of rain has already fallen.

There is no doubt that rules, policies and guidelines can help reduce risks, as they can keep the factors separate from one another. For example, a policy of no kayaking in the Buller River with novice 4th form groups eliminates the potential for an incident or accident happening during this activity. To be effective however rules must be specific and not ambiguous. To be relevant they must be clearly tied in with educational objectives for the programme.

EMPLOYING AN APPROPRIATE LEADERSHIP STYLE

Many books have been written on the subject of leadership styles. In an outdoor adventure-based programme setting, choosing the right style of leadership for different situations can be crucial to risk reduction.

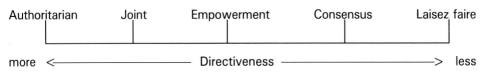

Fig. 13:   Leadership styles

Moving from a less directive style of leadership to a more directive style in some situations can reduce certain risks. For example to reduce risks it is sometimes appropriate to **tell** your group to:

> - put on a lifejacket for kayaking
> - ride their bikes slowly over rocky ground
> - keep away from crevasse edges.

This will work more effectively however, if the directive style is not used all the time and it is accompanied by clear explanations of why these directions must be followed.

A more directive style of leadership has advantages in a crisis situation when time is of the essence and peoples' skills must be directed exactly where they are needed.

Moving from a more directive style to a less directive style will have advantages in other situations. For example, group members will be more likely to share their medical conditions, fear and anxieties with an approachable less authoritarian leader. A group will be happier to abide by certain decisions on a tramping trip if they have been reached by consensus e.g. if there is a wide range of fitness in the party and the choice must be made between an easier or more difficult route.

There is little if no place for a leader responsible for a group to have a laissez faire approach to leadership. At the other extreme, an authoritarian leader may undermine their own leadership and alienate the group.

Leaders need to choose a style of leadership which they are comfortable with and be aware this may change with the changing demands and needs of the situation and the group.

(For more information about leadership and decision-making see NZMSC Bushcraft Manual).

KNOWING YOUR STUDENTS

The better you know your group, the more aware you are of their capabilities, individual needs, reactions to stress etc. If you are aware of these things you are less likely to put them into situations which are beyond them and where the risk level is too great. If you do **not** know your group very well before taking them on an outdoor activity, there are some excellent ways you can get to know them better before you go, or even before you begin the activity. Ice breaker games and activities, trust and problem solving activities can be effective methods of gaining immediate behavioural information about your group. It is well documented[2] that where there is an atmosphere of trust and looking after one another in a group, not only will the group and individuals reach higher goals but they will reach them in greater safety. Leaders who can facilitate this atmosphere are practising good risk management.

TEACHING BY PROGRESSION

Teaching by progression is teaching a skill by breaking it down into its component parts, and building on each part to increase the complexity of the task until an eventual goal is reached. For example, fig. 14 illustrates this concept exceptionally well in the activity of abseiling.

Fig. 14(a) & 14(b):   Abseiling

The effect of teaching in this way, is that the learner is progressively exposed to risk and hence feels less fear while learning the basic techniques of abseiling, e.g. body stance, hand positioning, use of abseil device, safety rope.

It is far easier for a person to concentrate and practice the techniques in relative ease when there is no gaping cliff behind them to distract their attention! Consequently the learner's confidence increases in relation to their skill.

It is up to the instructor to determine an appropriate progression for a given activity based on accepted standards of practice, then to tailor it to the needs of the particular venue, individual or group. Instructors must also remember that within any group, individuals will progress at different rates, so treating everyone equally with respect to levels of fear and rates of learning, does just about everyone an injustice.[3]

DEVELOPING SAFETY CONSCIOUSNESS

As a leader gains more experience working with groups in the outdoors, there is usually a corresponding increase in their safety consciousness and awareness. It is crucial that all outdoor leaders never stop learning or questioning. The leader in the picture is one we should all walk away from (or send on a Risk Management Course!).

Safety consciousness is not something you can pass (like a driving test) or pull out (like a pocket knife). It is an ongoing process of continually evaluating, applying skills and knowledge to new and changing situations, and exercising good **judgement** to reduce the chances of incidents and accidents happening before they have a chance to develop. Exercising good judgement can be a real juggling act!

HAVING THE PERSONAL SKILLS APPROPRIATE TO THE ACTIVITY

It goes without saying that leaders should have the personal skills appropriate to the activity they are instructing. This is an extremely effective way of reducing risks!

Some skills are specific to an activity, e.g.

kayaking:
- wet exit
- sweep strokes
- support strokes
- draw strokes
- eskimo roll.

Other skills are transferable across activities e.g.
- conflict resolution
- crisis management
- group management.

Having the appropriate skills for an activity should go hand-in-hand with the ability to accurately assess your own limitations and strengths. This process can be assisted by feedback from peers. (Chapter 5 looks at using self-assessment and peer feedback methods to assist leaders toward more accurate self-assessment).

A leader should strive to keep a good safety margin between the skills of the learners and their own skills. Example:

A Grade 2 + kayaking instructor who, after teaching a suitable progression of skills, takes a group of teenagers down a Grade 2 river may have trouble coping if something goes wrong. A Grade 4 paddler in the same situation however will have no trouble coping if an emergency arises.

Chapter 4, page 50 looks at the competence/difficulty module, a useful tool to assist an instructor to determine their appropriate mode of operation.

DISCLOSING THE RISK

This is a very important technique for reducing risks. It keys party members into risks which they may not be aware of because of lack of experience and then gives them tactics to deal with these risks. The following are some examples of risk disclosure:

(A) On a tramping trip there is always a risk of someone getting separated from the party and going the wrong way, leading to a night out in bad weather. To reduce this risk:

- tell your party about it.
- tell the group exactly **where** they will be tramping to for the day, and give them maps
- let them know **what** they should do if they are separated from the party.

(B) When using a stove there is always a risk of serious injury if it is used incorrectly, so:

- explain this risk to the group

then • give them instruction and let them practice **how** to light a stove before they need to use it.

(C) When an accident happens there is always the risk of the effects being made worse because the group has a confused response to the accident. Firstly:

• explain this risk to the group

• let everyone know **who** is carrying emergency equipment, and **who** has first aid skills in the party.

Risk disclosure not only reduces the chances of chaos reigning if something happens or complications developing (through ignorance) as a result, but merely giving information to the group will actually reduce the level of risk perceived by some group members. 'The greater the perceived risk in the situation, the greater the individual's felt need for information. In practice, this means the instructor can create feelings of anxiety and fear by merely withholding information.'[4]

Effective risk disclosure as an integral part of an outdoor journey or experience can also enhance learning opportunities for people and have the effect of empowering them for the future. By all counts, it will reduce the chances of the following type of incident occurring:

A youth group out for a day tramp in the Waitakere Ranges (Auckland), is travelling up river, scrambling along a track above the river bed. Two people are barefooted, two are in sandals, and some others are in sandshoes. The leader slips, knocks his head on a rock, and falls into the river unconscious, clutching the only map. The map floats away. No other leaders are with the group. The group has no idea where they are as they were not told in the first place.

Summary

Some effective ways of **reducing risks** are:
- having appropriate rules and policies
- employing appropriate leadership styles
- knowing your students
- teaching by progression
- developing safety consciousness
- having the personal skills appropriate to the activity
- disclosing the risk.

SOCIAL AND PSYCHOLOGICAL FACTORS

In addition to the more easily defined risk management principles outlined above, there are a set of well documented social and psychological factors which can contribute to risk. They can permeate an activity at various stages of its progression and also lead to accidents. These factors are at play whenever we take part in an outdoor activity, some at the beginning, some in the middle and some at the end of it. Making people aware that these factors exist and affect an individual's evaluation of risk, is the key to reducing their effect on subsequent decision-making.

Research has shown that social and psychological factors are high on the list of contributing factors of accidents. Two studies[5] revealed three items which clearly indicate that accepting increased levels of risk contributes to most accidents. They were, in order of priority: **risk shift, get home-itis and familiarisation with the situation**. The studies concluded that these were the three largest contributing factors to accidents.

In addition to these phenomena, such factors as **dropping your guard** and **attribution theory** contribute significantly to the causes of accidents and incidents also. For this reason, it is essential for leaders to be conscious of them, if they are to learn how to manage them effectively.

FAMILIARIZATION WITH THE SITUATION AND 'IT CAN'T HAPPEN TO ME'

The two studies[6] above also found that the great majority of serious injuries and fatalities were preceded within one year by a near miss or accident of a parallel nature in the same area. This seems to imply that in spite of an accident or near miss, the group leadership failed to perceive that it could happen to them. This was the **third largest contributing factor in accidents** and is probably a result of **familiarisation with the situation**, where continued exposure to a hazard in a frequently used area reduced the leader/s perception of risks associated with the hazards. Previous accidents or near misses could have been seen as freak or chance events, or perhaps repeated exposure to a hazard simply made people more insensitive to it.

The following is an extreme example to illustrate this point. While on Mt Everest, British climber Chris Bonington wrote about being conditioned to danger.

'Entering the ice fall has an element of Russian roulette. There is no possibility of making a safe route . . . all you can do is pick out a route which is as safe as possible, but there will always be sections which are threatened by ice towers which, sooner or later, must collapse.'

A few days later, Bonington understood the effects of exposure to continuous danger.

'It is strange how one's attitude to a route through a glacier or icefall changes. The first time through, one's progress is slow and nerve-racking, but once the route is made, even though it gets no safer, one treats the glacier in an increasingly blasé manner . . .'

In effect, **familiarization with a situation** leads to an attitude of 'it can't happen to me'. This in turn can result in **dropping your guard**, which can actually lower your perception of the risks involved. In an outdoor situation, particularly when you have responsibility for others, your guard must be kept up at all times, as dropping it could have dire consequences in some situations.

RISK SHIFT

A social aspect of risk taking which should concern outdoor educators is the well documented **Risk Shift Phenomenon.**
'Groups make riskier decisions than the individuals that comprise them'.[7]

"PERHAPS MAYBE A LITTLE TO THE RIGHT NOW "

This can occur on a trip when the going gets tough. Individuals within the group become increasingly unsure about how they are going to cope and wish to turn back. Each one is however reluctant to be the one to suggest turning back so the trip continues. During discussion, group members with more knowledge or experience induce a riskier decision from the less experienced. This happens when individuals who realise they are less bold than others in the group adjust their risk-taking attitudes upwards.

One of the explanations for **risk shift** is that risk is of social value and risk taking is a socially valued behaviour. It is no wonder then that the individuals in the above group were reluctant to be seen as conservative when the valued behaviour was to be daring. So in risk-taking situations the bolder members of the group are often the most influential.[8] Another manifestation of **risk shift** is when a person within a group abandons responsibility for him/herself and places this responsibility onto someone else in the group, usually the leader or another skilled person. This often takes place without the leader or skilled person's knowledge. The leader or group therefore is not necessarily keeping a special watch on that person, or offering them extra support and the person is reluctant to admit to being out of their depth because they want to appear to be coping. The consequences of **risk shift** can put not only the person but the whole group at risk. For example:

> A tramping party finds out halfway across a river that one person has never crossed a river before. The person panics and as a result the party breaks up in swift water. The inexperienced person drowns while the rest of the party manages to packfloat to safety.

A review of research[9] stated:

> 'Taking risks indicates courage and forcefulness, and is generally more highly valued than conservatism. Most people, particularly men, tend to respect and admire others who are willing to take risks. Being in a group reinforces the importance of the social desirability and thus tends to make individuals move towards the more desirable, risky alternative.'[10]

Two studies[11] show the risk shift phenomena **to be the largest contributing cause to accidents**.

DROPPING YOUR GUARD

Dropping your guard, although linked to **get home-itis** and **familiarisation with the situation**, has its own characteristics.

> It was the end of the week at 4th form camp. The group had been through thick and thin together. They had 'jelled' together on the overnight tramp, and individuals had pushed themselves on the confidence course and other activities. The culmination of the whole week was to get the whole team over 'the wall'. They used their planning time effectively then began to put their ideas into practice. Everyone was involved in maximum support, spotting, lifting or hoisting member by member over the 12ft featureless slab. Half the team was over. The next person, Lisa, was assisted up and over by people on the ground and on top of the wall. Some tense moments, and she was there. Relieved, the team reorganised for the next person.
>
> Lisa, legs still trembling, began the climb down. Team energy was now focussed on the next to go over, when a scream, followed by a thump and groan came from behind the wall. Lisa had slipped and fallen from a height of 6ft on the downside of the wall — injuring her arm on the way down. This is an example of 'dropping your guard'. Maximum support and safety was given on the way up, but when she was up, all attention shifted to the next person and Lisa also relaxed her concentration (dropped her guard) on the way down, leading to the accident.

The same thing can happen in a mountaineering situation on the **return** from the climb.

GET HOME-ITIS

Get home-itis, can result from trying to adhere to a schedule or simply forgetting everything else once the end is in sight. This is another social and psychological phenomena which affects the levels of risk accepted by an individual or group at the end of an outdoor experience.

For example:

(A) A primary class is at the local park observing the spectrum of autumn colours. The activity has gone overtime and several children pressure the teacher to allow them to return to school on their own as they have lunch order duties. They are allowed to go. Other children see these children go, and stop the activity and wander off too. Before long ⅓ of the class is making their way back to school (1 block) and the teacher, realising she has an appointment, sends the rest of the class back to school unattended while she heads off to school at a very quick pace. This is in contrast to the orderly controlled manner in which they walked to the park. Two children are not in class at 1 pm, they were last seen talking to a stranger in the park at the end of the activity.

(b) A youth club tramping party of two adults and six students, on the last day of their weekend tramp, come to a swollen river one hour before the road end. The weather had deteriorated the night before and it has been raining steadily all day.

The party is due back home that evening and at school the next day. Everyone is wet and tired, but determined to get back to the car, a hot shower and a roof over their heads.

The leaders decide to give the crossing a go, as they have no tents, and it is three hours back to the hut; besides, the parents will be **worried sick** if they don't turn up tonight.

These are both cases of **get home-itis,** and the result of psychological and social pressure to get home which is perceived as so important that additional risks and hazards diminish compared to the importance of the goal. In the two studies[12] mentioned **this was the second largest contributing cause to accidents.**

ATTRIBUTION THEORY

A basic understanding of attribution theory can help us understand our behaviour in certain outdoor situations. The attribution process deals with the human tendency to take credit for positive behaviours or outcomes but to deny responsibility for bad or negative ones.[13] This stems from a strong desire to protect our self-esteem and reflects our desire to present a positive public image. For example:

An orienteering team will account for their wins at a national event largely in terms of internal causes (e.g. their group's high ability, its heroic efforts). In contrast they are much more likely to attribute their losses to external factors (e.g. faulty compass, poorly set up course, bad weather).

Because people are unwilling to accept responsibility for bad or negative situations which occur it can be difficult to find out the real cause of accidents and near misses and to put measures in place to reduce the chances of similar events happening again.

Take the example of the teacher who has poor navigation skills and no desire to disclose this to staff or students. The group gets lost for several hours, walks three to four hours longer than necessary and great stress is experienced by all during the whole exercise. At the end of the trip the teacher blames the incident on the lack of a clear sign at the beginning of the track. A sign is put up but the teacher's poor map reading and navigation skills and reluctance to disclose this remains unchanged.

There is a real need in outdoor education in New Zealand to separate responsibility from blame. We may not be to **blame** for many situations which happen in the outdoors, but we **all** have the **responsibility** to acknowledge the true causes and take action to reduce the chances of them happening again.

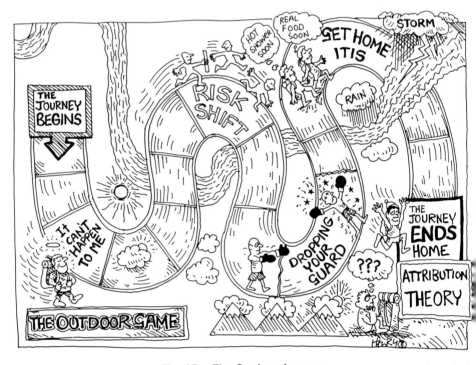

Fig. 15: The Outdoor Journey
Social and psychological factors to watch out for along your way.

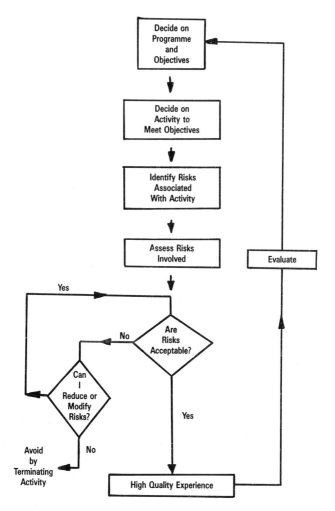

Fig. 16: Implementing risk management principles into your planning process

SUMMARY

An **awareness** and understanding of the principles of risk management discussed in this section are essential for effective management of risks in outdoor activities. They have been well analysed through research and indeed many have been taken into consideration by outdoor leaders and instructors over the years. These principles will form the basis of the rest of this manual.

TOOLS
What are the tools for managing risks?

PLANNING TOOLS

Some useful tools have been developed to help leaders manage risks in the outdoors.

THE RISK ANALYSIS AND MANAGEMENT SYSTEM— RAMS

The original risk management planning matrix[1] was developed in 1987 by a group of outdoor educators as a checklist for planning activities in the outdoors. It was also adapted for use as an evaluation tool. Grant Davidson has adapted this system to its present form.

Risk management can be thought of in terms of priority areas. The priorities can be likened to those in first aid. In first aid the priority areas are A, B, C (Airway, Breathing, Circulation).

The key areas to focus on in risk management are:

— **people, resources and equipment, environment.**

All of these areas are associated with a particular activity.

Planning to minimise risks in these three areas involves going through a number of stages:

— Risk identification
  What are the potential risks and causal factors associated with each area?

— Risk management
  What strategies can be put into place to manage them?

— Coping with emergencies
  What back-up is necessary should any of the risks be realised?

Fig. 17: Risk Analysis Management System (RAMS) form
(See back of book for photocopy master of this form).

RELEVANT INDUSTRY STANDARDS APPLICABLE	
POLICIES AND GUIDELINES RECOMMENDED	
SKILLS REQUIRED BY STAFF	
FINAL DECISION ON IMPLEMENTING ACTIVITY	<u>Choose one</u> Accept ✓ Reject Comments:

RISK ANALYSIS AND MANAGEMENT SYSTEM

NAME: _____   DATE: _____

ACTIVITY/SITUATION: _____

Analysis   Description

		People	Equipment	Environment
RISKS	Accident, injury other forms loss			
CAUSAL FACTORS	Hazards, perils, dangers			
RISK MANAGEMENT STRATEGIES	Normal Operation			
	Emergency			

© Grant Davidson 1992

40

How to use the RAMS (See Fig. 17)

1. Identify the accidents or incidents (risks) you are hoping to avoid. Number these if you wish.

2. For each risk identified list the **causal factors** which could lead up to it under the headings people, equipment, environment. It can be helpful to number these to correspond with the above.

3. For each of the **causal factors**, work out a strategy which will reduce the risk to an acceptable level.

   For each of the causal factors, adopt one of the following management techniques:
   - reduce
   - avoid
   - transfer
   - retain.

   When considering options to reduce the risk refer to Chapter 3, pages 27-33.

   You now have a plan for your **normal operation**.

4. The final stage of your risk management planning involves pre-planning emergency strategies. Here you need to formulate a plan for coping with each of the initially identified risks, should they be realised.

Flipside of RAMS form

The flipside of the RAMS form can be used to put your plan into a larger context i.e. where does your planned activity fit in terms of current industry standards, organisation policies and guidelines, and what are the skills required by your staff?

This process should help you or your administrators decide whether your activity should or should not go ahead.

Relevant Industry Standards for the outdoors can be found in Guidelines for Outdoor Educators, NZMSC Manuals, NZCA Handbook, NZOIA Syllabi, as well as many other publications. (See references pages 101-104). A code of practice is currently being developed for Education Outside the Classroom. (See Appendix A for details).

These are intended as national guidelines of sound professional practice accepted within our industry.

Ways of using the RAMS

The RAMS is a useful planning format to help ensure nothing important is missed out. It can be an excellent tool for organising your thoughts into the key areas, before an activity and it can also provide a useful focal point for several people planning the same activity. They can 'brainstorm' through it together, identifying common, clear objectives and strategies as well as sorting out individual responsibilities.

The RAMS can also be used as source documents for an organisation's policies and guidelines and staff training requirements for specific activities. In this case the polices and guidelines become recommended management strategies for the section on the first page of the form, as do the skills required by staff.

Any policy contained in an organisation's staff handbook should be able to be traced to the appropriate RAMS analysis as a risk reduction method for a specific identified risk and causal factor.

Samples of completed RAMS forms follow:

A: The visit to the fire station discussed in Chapter 3, pages 18 and 19.

B: A trust fall activity.

RISK ANALYSIS AND MANAGEMENT SYSTEM

NAME: Ms Black   DATE: 5.11.92

ACTIVITY/SITUATION: Visit to the Fire Station—pre-school group

Analysis   Description

RISKS Accident, injury, other forms loss		1. Child injured around equipment, engines 2. Psychological damage—fear of fire engines 3. Process of learning impaired.		
CAUSAL FACTORS Hazards, perils, dangers		**People**	**Equipment**	**Environment**
		Poor supervision around engine or machinery. Children with medical problems eg. asthma. Confusion and panic due to children in the way. Poor briefing of helpers. Unsuitable helpers.	Siren goes off whilst group is at station. Children small compared to size of engines. Car breaks down.	Stimulating environment could distract attention. Siren noise could panic children. Confined space.
RISK MANAGEMENT STRATEGIES	Normal Operation	Helpers well briefed on responsibilities. Children supervised well around machinery. Use of medical forms. Plan most suitable areas for group to view engines—where out of way. View engines *not* on call.	Children assisted to climb on engines when necessary. Contingency plan for car problems: all drivers given station phone number. Brief children on possibility of siren going off and what to do.	Ensure children can explore the station where they are not in way. Brief children about siren noise and what to do—practice if possible. Restrict numbers of children in confined areas.
	Emergency	Have first aid kit on hand. Teacher qualified in first aid. Teacher skilled at class supervision and communication to handle emergency. School has prepared emergency procedures. Pre-visit the site to personally check it out and meet staff.		

© *Grant Davidson, 1992*

Fig. 18(a):   Completed RAMS form—visit to fire station

RELEVANT INDUSTRY STANDARDS APPLICABLE	"Principals Guide to Education Outside the Classroom' recommends a ratio of 1:8 on this type of excursion.
POLICIES AND GUIDELINES RECOMMENDED	Pre-school recommends ratio of 1:4. Staff must pre-visit the site. Vehicles involved in transport must all be fitted with seatbelts and cars must not be overloaded. Carry first aid kit. Maximum 20 in group. Emergency plans on file.
SKILLS REQUIRED BY STAFF	Teachers must hold current First Aid Certificate. Taken groups on excursions before, or with more experienced staff.

FINAL DECISION ON IMPLEMENTING ACTIVITY	Choose one
	Accept ✔ Reject
	Comments: Stimulating experience for children to get to know their community. Safe with precautions listed above in place.

Fig. 18(b): Completed RAMS form (flipside) - visit to fire station.

43

RISK ANALYSIS AND MANAGEMENT SYSTEM

NAME: <u>Instructor Jones</u>   DATE: <u>22/3/92</u>

ACTIVITY/SITUATION: <u>Trust Fall Initiative Exercise at Camp</u>

Analysis   Description

RISKS Accident, injury other forms loss	1. Faller hits ground from height and is injured. 2. Catchers are injured during the exercise. 3. Students do not want to take part in activity. 4. Faller is emotionally or socially damaged in activity, preventing participation in future events.

	People	**Equipment**	**Environment**
CAUSAL FACTORS Hazards, perils, dangers	Taught poor catching technique. Taught poor falling technique. Poor communication. Poor group control. Too few catchers. Too many participants. Students have special needs (fears, anxieties, etc). Students medical problems.	Inappropriate take-off point — too high — insecure — too uneven. Inappropriate clothing. Students wearing jewellery, watches, glasses, etc.	Uneven terrain for catchers. Slippery terrain. Weather unsuitable.

		People	**Equipment**	**Environment**
RISK MANAGEMENT STRATEGIES	**Normal Operation**	Instructor aware of correct catching and falling techniques. Instructor skilled at communication. Instructor skilled at group control. Set minimum number in group. Set maximum number in group. Have knowledge of group. Disclose risks and precautions. Use catching technique that is gender sensitive. Use medical forms for participants to disclose history. Allow challenge by choice.	Choose appropriate take-off point. Check if secure. Have loose clothing tucked in. Remove jewellery, glasses, etc.	Choose site that is flat. Check weather, past and present. Be prepared to change activities if weather changes. Dress for weather. Check students dress.
	Emergency	Have first aid kit at hand. Instructor qualified in first aid skills. Instructor skilled at group skills and communication to handle emergency. Organisation has prepared an emergency plan for injuries/accidents. Take spare clothing if appropriate.		

© *Grant Davidson,* 1992

Fig. 19(a): Completed RAMS form for trust fall activity

44

RELEVANT INDUSTRY STANDARDS APPLICABLE	Project Adventure—recommend a progression of trust activities leading up to the trust fall. AEE—recommend participants remove jewellery and objects from pockets. Glasses should be retained by straps. Staff should explain group goals and dangers. Technique should involve catchers' hands zippered not held: leads to dislocation. Recommend that the fall is from a height no greater than that of the catchers' elbows.
POLICIES AND GUIDELINES RECOMMENDED	Instructors to have observed the exercise carried out by a senior member of staff previously. The take-off point should be no higher than shoulder-height: elbow-height better. Minimum of eight catchers in the group. Maximum of 16 people in group. Carry first aid kit. Emergency plans on file.
SKILLS REQUIRED BY STAFF	Instructors first aid certified. Trained in group dynamics and communications skills. Observed initiative exercises before.

FINAL DECISION ON IMPLEMENTING ACTIVITY	Choose one	
	Accept ✔	Reject
	Comments: Safe and challenging activity with precautions listed above.	

Fig. 19(b): Completed RAMS form (flipside) for trust fall activity

45

DIFFERENT FORMATS

The most important element in effective risk management planning is to ensure that the **principles** of risk management have been considered. The RAMS is certainly not the only format for doing this. Many outdoor leaders incorporate the principles into their own styles of planning and running activities in the outdoors.

For example, here are:

Some thoughts on Risk Management skills applied to river crossing on a trip[2]

1. **Identifying the Risk:**
   — Drowning
   — Hypothermia
   — Psychological damage
   — Loss of equipment

2. **Causal Factors:**
   Environment:
   — What type of river is it?
     (gorge, shingle, boulders)
   — How fast is the current?
   — How cold is the water?
   — What is the river bottom like?
   — Are there any snags apparent?
   — Are there any eddies which might be used?
   — What are the entry and exit points like?
   — What is the run-out like?
   — Are banks steep?
   — Are there any other hazards?
   — Is there a bridge or cableway with less real risk?
   — What is the weather like? (air temperature, precipitation)
   — Is the river going to rise or fall?

People:
— What experience do the people in your party have?
— How do they feel about doing the crossing?
— Are there stronger members of the team?
— Are there weaker members of the team?
— Are they cold or tired already?

Equipment:
— Is everyone adequately clothed for the crossing? (warm clothing, boots, etc.)
— What equipment do we have which might be of use? (packs, logs, etc.)
— What equipment do we have which might be a hindrance?

3. **Reduction of Risk:**
Trip planning:
— Have you chosen the best route?
— Is there a better place to cross?
— Is it possible to avoid crossing?
— Have you researched local conditions/knowledge?

Leadership:
— Do you know your group well?
— Have you adopted the appropriate leadership style for the party?
— Have you assessed the real risk appropriately?
— How much of the risk should you disclose to the party?

Personal skills:
— Have you a wide experience of the crossing techniques yourself?
— What method of crossing should you use? (mutual support, pole, individual)
— Is this the best time of the day to cross? (glacial rivers)
— Have you chosen a good spot?
  • run out
  • speed
  • depth
  • entry and exit
— Have you anticipated all the problems?
— Does your group have a good understanding of safety consciousness?
— Does each member of your group know what to do if something goes wrong?

4. **Real and Perceived Risk (Assessment of Risk):**
The checklist above will give some indication of the assessment of real risk, when combined with a background of experience in various crossing situations.

The decision of whether the risk in crossing is justified will come down to your judgement of **conditions present, party conditions (physical and psychological)** based on long personal experience and observation.

Before Practical Session

Check

Individual equipment	—polypropylene or woollen gear
	—wet suit
	—socks, boots and sand shoes
	—pack some gear in pack
	—plastic bags
	—towel
	—extra warm clothes
Group gear	—life jackets
	—a large pole
	—individual pole for each group member
	—1 billy, 1 primus, soup, tea or coffee
	—1 first aid kit
	—helmets

There are many ways of incorporating risk management principles into your planning style whether you are new to leading people in the outdoors, or whether you have had vast experience. Different ways suit different people. The above are some ideas. The first step is awareness, the rest is up to you.

EVALUATION TOOLS

THE RAMS AS AN EVALUATION TOOL

The RAMS can also be used as an effective evaluation tool for an activity. It can help identify key areas where improvements could be made and the most appropriate ways to achieve them. It can also help highlight the areas where risks were managed most effectively.

The following is an example of a RAMS used in this way, to evaluate an orienteering event around the school grounds.

RISK ANALYSIS AND MANAGEMENT SYSTEM

NAME: Mr Zed/Ms White   DATE: 7/5/93

ACTIVITY/SITUATION: ORIENTEERING

Analysis   **Description**

RISKS Accident, injury other forms loss		

CAUSAL FACTORS Hazards, perils, dangers	**People**	**Equipment**	**Environment**
	<u>Improvements</u> Cheating was a problem—next time have clippers instead of clues to copy down.	<u>Improvements</u> Clippers next time instead of clues.	<u>Improvements</u> Boundaries need to be more clearly set e.g. lay down rules: —No running inside —No crossing roads as these are out of bounds.

RISK MANAGEMENT STRATEGIES

Normal / Operation

What went well	**Went well**	**Went well**

The buddy system of 1 experienced with 1 inexperienced forming the pairs.	Maps—clear
	   —coloured
	   —accurate
	Placement of markers right level for group.
	First Aid kit present.
	Base in central location.
		Ideal area
		—variety of terrain
		—clear boundaries.

Emergency

<u>General</u>   A successful event. Students enjoyed it. Most scored well. Easy for staff with little experience to set up and run.

© Grant Davidson, 1992

Fig. 20: RAMS used as an evaluation tool for an orienteering event

49

OPERATION ZONES

The competence/difficulty model for adventure activities (see fig. 21) is a useful tool to help determine the balance which must be sought when assessing the risks associated with a particular activity for a particular group.

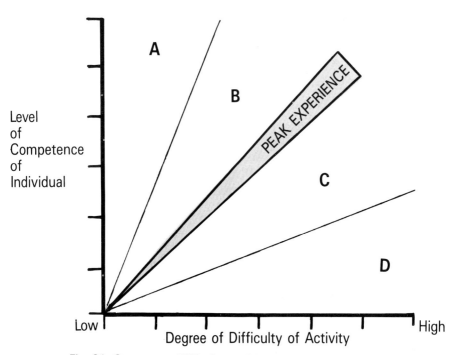

COMPETENCE/DIFFICULTY MODEL
FOR ADVENTURE ACTIVITIES

Fig. 21: Competence/difficulty model for adventure activities
(Davidson 1992 adapted from McConnell 1989, Priest & Baillie 1987)

The operation zones described below, although broad, illustrate potential danger zones and safety zones.

A — Play: The skill level of the participant is far in excess of the degree of difficulty of the activity. There is no challenge or excitement. This can lead to boredom, a lack of concentration and to accidents.

B — Cruising: Skill level is above the degree of difficulty of the activity and participants can cope easily with challenges or emergencies. Enjoyment without stress.

C—Challenge:	The degree of difficulty of the activity is slightly above participants' skill levels. Maximum concentration is required, there may be some anxiety or excitement and there is potential for mishap.
D—Distress:	The degree of difficulty is way above the skill level of the participants. Anxiety and fear can lead to mishaps, serious accident and injury or even death.
Peak experience:	This is the zone where people's competence matches the difficulty of the task best. It is the zone where participants can experience the euphoric state mentioned in Chapter 2, page 9. It is often the ultimate goal of an adventure-based programme.

The competence/difficulty model can help an outdoor leader determine the right level of activity for a particular group. Example (see Fig. 22):

A group of 10 students plus two staff on a kayak trip.
— three pupils are paddling flat water and grade 1 competently
— six pupils are paddling grade 2
— one pupil is just capable of paddling grade 3
— two staff are paddling grade 3-4 competently.

COMPETENCE/DIFFICULTY MODEL
FOR A KAYAK TRIP

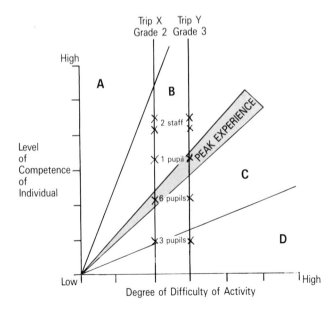

Fig. 22:   Competence/difficulty model for a kayak trip

On trip X:
Although they will get their challenge from managing the group, the staff will be operating in the upper B zone—Cruising, one pupil will be operating in B zone—Cruising, six pupils will be operating in the peak experience zone, three pupils will be operating in C zone—Challenge. They will find it **very** challenging/bordering on distress.

On trip Y:
The staff will be operating in the lower B zone—Cruising, one pupil will be operating in the peak experience zone, six pupils will be operating in C zone—Challenge, and three pupils will be operating in D zone—Distress.

It does not take an expert to decide which is the more suitable trip for this particular group as a whole.

Trip 'X' might be suitable for this group in the right conditions i.e. river normal, fine weather, water not too cold, adequate gear etc. It must be noted that for three of the group it will be a real challenge. Leaders must expect 'can outs' and have strategies to cope. With adequate risk management planning and good emergency procedures in place it could be a 'peak' experience for the group.

Trip 'Y' however, is beyond the resources of this group.

Points to note:
- There can be a range of ability within one group.
- The activity (or trip) chosen should be within the capabilities of everyone involved.
- The leader must be extremely competent in the chosen activity because if they find it a challenge they will be of little or no help if others get into trouble i.e. there will be no safety margin.
- The leader should seek their challenge in managing the group, not from the activity itself.

This competence/difficulty model can also be used to evaluate a trip and learn from it, as happened with the following trip:

Two friends were planning to do a trip over the Copeland Pass in the school summer holidays. Bob, the leader, had extensive climbing experience and Peter had extensive tramping experience at both bush and alpine levels. Other members of the party would be Bob's wife, Jane, and another friend, Jim, who had both done a lot of tramping and would be challenged by this alpine trip. Planning went ahead. Shortly before the trip began Jim talked Bob into letting his wife Naomi (who he said had tramping experience) join the party. Jim then persuaded Naomi to accompany them, playing down the difficulty of the trip.

On the trip it quickly became apparent that Naomi had done very limited tramping and had come along only to please her husband. She needed constant encouragement and physical assistance which held the whole party up. On reaching the top of the pass Naomi sat down and refused to go any further or back the way they had come. She was quite distressed, frightened and totally out of her depth. It took several hours of cajoling, encouragement and worry on everyone else's part to persuade Naomi to start moving again. The party finally made it down to shelter rocks on the West Coast side for a late bivvy. Luckily the weather was favourable throughout. The trip was the most stressful the leader had ever encountered and was such a horrific experience for Naomi she never wanted to tramp again.

Let's see how this party fits onto the model:

COMPETENCE/DIFFICULTY MODEL
FOR A TRIP OVER THE COPELAND PASS

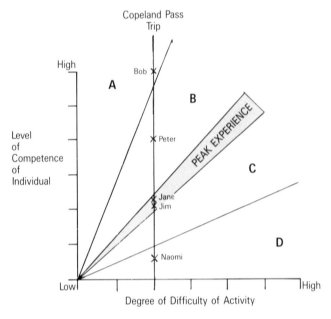

Fig. 23: Competence/difficulty model for a trip over the Copeland Pass

On this trip, rated as a two on the difficulty scale, the skills in the party ranged from 5→1:
- Bob was operating in A Zone – Plenty of experience to be leading this trip.
- Peter was operating in B Zone – Well within his capabilities.
- Jane and Jim were operating in Peak Experience zone – A challenge for them.
- Naomi was operating in D Zone – In a state of distress for most of the trip.

At the end of the trip, the leader vowed never to take an 'unknown' on a trip again as not only had the trip been a negative experience for Naomi, but for the whole party. Naomi's state of distress also put everyone else at risk. If they had encountered bad weather at the top of the Pass, the party could have got into real difficulty. This trip could be described as a near miss.

53

CHAPTER 5

SELF-ASSESSMENT AND PEER FEEDBACK
How well do you assess yourself, your group and the risks involved?

GENERAL

Self-examination and assessment, assisted by peer feedback, is fundamental to the process of becoming familiar with sound risk management practices. The aim of self-assessment and peer feedback is for the leader of the activity to get to know and understand themselves better so they can make sound judgements in the outdoors.

Why self-assessment and peer feedback?

SELF

Individuals learn best if they are involved in the assessment process. This means reflecting on:

— where they are at
— their performance to date
— their feelings
— the impact their actions have on others
— what they set out to do.

PEERS

Peers are usually those people in the same age group, involved in the same occupation or activities.

Those in the same peer group, whether they work under, alongside or above, can assist an individual to self-realisation. They can provide **feedback** to help refine a person's own self-assessment.

Through self-assessment and peer feedback individuals can come to know themselves better.

MODEL

For the above process to be emotionally safe (non-threatening) and successful, it is best to use an appropriate feedback model and a trained facilitator. The risk management training and assessment packages which have been developed by Education, the NZ Mountain Safety Council and the Hillary Commission, incorporate self-assessment and peer feedback to assist in more accurate self-knowledge — psychological and emotional safety are important in this process. To this end all schemes now use trained facilitators and a self-assessment and peer feedback model developed from the work of John Heron.[1] This model has been adapted to the needs of individuals and groups both giving and receiving feedback and assessing themselves. Certain ground rules underpin the feedback procedure and the whole process is designed to provide security, honesty, confidentiality, affirmation and a refined self-assessment for all involved.

WHAT PEOPLE HAVE SAID ABOUT SELF-ASSESSMENT AND PEER FEEDBACK?

'I have gained personal confidence from the activities and the debriefing [feedback] model.'

'I feel this concept is an immensely valuable and supportive method of making constructive criticism as well as positive praise.'

'Many personal gains, e.g. Better overall view of 'self' thanks to peer and self assessment. A list of ideas for further personal growth.'

'Structured sessions were frustrating for me and others initially. But the 'advice' first, 'positives' second was accepted and allowed great growth. It does offer the individuals security when focussing directly on them . . . Know my limitations (where I'm at). Have ideas of where to implement changes.'

'A facilitation process that works — it is relatively non threatening and positively constructive.'[2]

Note: More about this feedback model may be found out by attending a risk management course. Courses available range from one and two day introductory courses to five day experiential ones.[3] (See References, page 104 for course contacts). The whole self-assessment and peer feedback process is based on the risk management principles outlined in Chapter 3 and the tools for risk management discussed in Chapter 4.

LOGBOOKS

The process of self-assessment should be seen as an ongoing, lifelong process for the outdoor leader. Learning does not stop once you begin to lead activities. In many ways, it is just beginning. It is widely acknowledged and emphasised that experience is the best way to gain skills appropriate to leading groups in the outdoors, and a **LOGBOOK** is one way of recording accumulated experience.

Outdoor educators and leaders are now encouraged to keep a **record** of their experiences in the outdoors in the form of an **outdoor logbook**. This can be an excellent tool for ongoing self-assessment as it can help you keep up-to-date, identify weak areas and encourage you to plan how to strengthen each area.

For example there are many ways a leader can gain the appropriate skills to lead activities outdoors:

— go along on activities in an assistant's role to learn from more experienced leaders
— go on a suitable training course

   e.g.
- Bushcraft
- Risk Management
- Education Outside the Classroom
- First Aid
- Science Outdoors
- Group Facilitation

— build up experience through personal recreation; tramping, botany field trips, caving
— seek opportunities to lead groups on activities within your own personal capabilities.

Most logged experience, such as the examples above, may be categorised under the following headings in your logbook:

- Personal outdoor experience (recreational)
- Training undertaken
- Instructional experience
- First Aid qualifications.

In the outdoors **everyone** is on a training path and a logbook provides a great way to map your future direction and record your journey so far. A generic logbook, which is supported and used by many outdoor agencies, is available from the NZ Mountain Safety Council. Other agencies have their own specialised logbooks.

CHAPTER 6

CRISIS MANAGEMENT
What if things go wrong?

IMAGERY

James Raffan[1] advocates images for crisis management. He believes that although all prudent outdoor leaders do first aid and rescue courses and become familiar with safety and risk management procedures, it is not long before much of the information is beyond quick recall. Hence he suggests it is useful to condense safety principles into **images** which can serve as constant reminders of safety and risk management details. This chapter will explore some imagery for visualising risk, risk management, the causes of accidents, and safety.

LEMONS

Remember the slot machine—the one armed bandit bolted to a tree? Remember too that every time you take a group outdoors you are putting a coin into the slot and pulling the handle down. Each time a causal factor is ignored, up pops a **lemon** in one of the windows. As more factors are overlooked, more lemons appear. The process continues until either you arrive at the end of the outdoor activity or you rack up enough lemons to hit the jackpot . . . **disaster**!

To illustrate, let's look at the NZ Mountain Safety Council's video on hypothermia, 'Such a Stupid Way to Die',[2] and spot the lemons.

- There was no-one on the trip who had the experience to be leading it.

- The victim did not have adequate clothing e.g. hat and parka.

- The Norwest arch, weather signs were ignored.

- The victim did not eat any breakfast.

- They party left the track to take a 'short cut' on the way back, were eventually bluffed on this route and had an exhausting climb back up to the ridge in deteriorating weather.

- The victim was given alcohol to warm up. (No food or extra clothing).

- The party pushed on back to the hut assisting the victim when he was unable to continue by himself.

- The party put the victim next to a fire to warm him up.

- The victim dies.

Fig. 24: Causal Factors: Such a Stupid Way to Die

The result of the **causal** factors (in fig. 24) being ignored was that the victim, Tom, died of hypothermia in the hut. To make the gambling metaphor work for you, ask yourself:

'Which incidents in my experience have been due to four and a half lemons coming up?'

'How many near misses have I got away with?'

Unwittingly, many outdoor educators take unnecessary risks. Are there any among us who have not had a close call? The first step in coming to terms with risk is to admit that an accident **can** happen to any one of us. Don't fall into the trap of thinking 'it can't happen to me'. The lemon analogy is similar to the simplified causal sequence (page 19) because it shows that an accident is not simply an unavoidable act of providence, but the logical consequence of a series of unmanaged factors. These are further compounded by carelessness, ignorance, short sightedness, bad judgements or at times outright arrogance. The word **'crisis'**, meaning *crucial turning point in a series of events*, better describes the situation.

Would things have been different:
— if the party leader/s had planned for such a possibility?
— if the victim's gear had been checked before they left home and he'd even borrowed a hat and parka?
— if he'd been required to eat breakfast that morning?
— if the party had heeded the warning signs in the weather and been prepared to return on the track they knew?
— if they had recognised the symptoms of hypothermia and knew how to treat it or prevent it occurring in the first place?

Things could have been very different if an experienced person had led this party but poor leadership meant that events progressed to a point where all chances of the victim surviving were eroded completely.

Individually, any one of these oversights (lemons) would not have had any serious bearing on the outcome of the tramping trip. It was when a number of factors were combined and compounded that the odds for disaster rose to 'inevitable' levels.[3]

COPING WITH CRISIS

Three major areas are interconnected to form a Crisis Management Triangle:

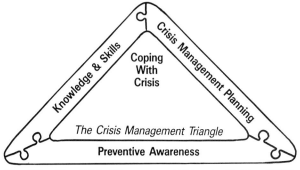

Fig. 25: The Crisis Management Triangle (Raffan 1984)

61

| Knowledge & skills | — Most outdoor leaders should have current knowledge and be proficient in outdoor skills. These include the activity skills, first aid, search and rescue and other safety techniques. This relates to the risk management principle of having the skills appropriate to the activity. |

| Preventive awareness | — is a continuous search for lemons and is tied into the risk management principles of knowing your students and developing safety consciousness. A constant hunt for lemons at the crisis stage helps prevent the crisis worsening and further crises developing. |

| Crisis management planning | — means preparing a **total plan** to deal with a possible crisis before it happens. The 'Coping with Emergencies' column on the RAMS form is for this stage of the planning. Practice sessions and simulations can be excellent ways of working out how best to deal with certain crises, (e.g. river rescue and first aid) so that quick action is paramount. |

CRISIS PROFILES

Confusion and disorganisation are usually the initial reaction to a crisis, people involved may refuse to believe they are faced with a crisis, or they may be suffering from shock. The situation is often made worse when unreasoned attempts are made to solve the crisis. The 'headless chook syndrome' may be operating here or the party may genuinely be unaware of the correct things to do as in 'Such a Stupid Way to Die' (see page 60).

In 'Such a Stupid Way to Die' the crisis, or crucial turning point was when the victim became slower and slower on his way back up to the ridge. Party members tried various solutions to the problem:

— talking to and encouraging him

— giving him alcohol

— shouting at him

— physically helping him (which pushed beyond his physical reserves)

— changing his wet clothes

— giving a hot drink

— rewarming him next to a fire.

The final outcome of the combination of these trial and error solutions was the victim's death.

By measuring the stress felt during a crisis, we can draw a picture of a typical crisis.

PROFILE OF A CRISIS

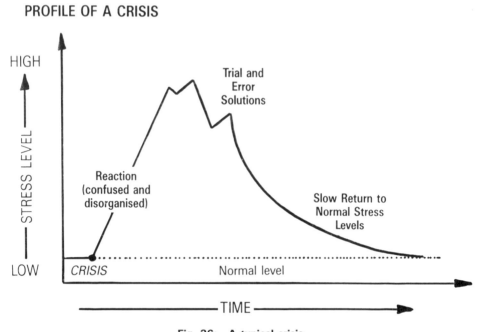

Fig. 26: A typical crisis

When the crisis happens there is a slow reaction time. More time is wasted with trial and error solutions, and a slow return to normal stress levels ensues once a solution is found to work.

Looking at the profile of a typical crisis (fig. 26) there are four obvious steps to be taken which could improve the situation:

1. Avoid the crisis in the first place through good risk management strategies.

2. Speed reaction time by having an emergency plan ready and the skills and experience to put it into action. The emergency section of the RAMS should contain this.

3. Reduce the number of trial and error solutions by organising the group to react and put the plan into action, preferably having already practiced it in a simulated situation.

4. Reduce the amount of time needed to resolve the crisis.

Implementation of these ideas would result in a new crisis profile (see fig. 27).

PROFILE OF A MANAGED CRISIS

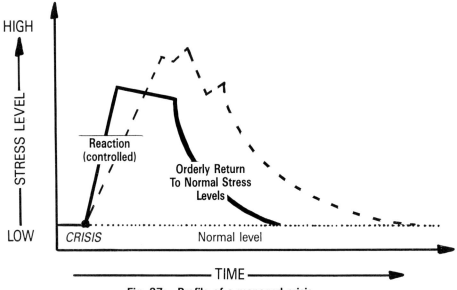

Fig. 27: Profile of a managed crisis

THE CRISIS RESOLUTION PLAN

The following five steps towards crisis resolution can help hasten a return to normal stress levels.

1. SEARCH	—	locating lost people.
2. RESCUE	—	removing a victim from a potentially life threatening location.
3. FIRST AID	—	treating victim/s for injuries, in the short and long terms.
4. EVACUATION	—	transportation of victim/s from the crisis location to professional health care.
	—	look after the rest of the party.
5. FOLLOW-UP	—	making sure the right authorities are notified of the crisis.
	—	implement any recommendations as a result of debriefing the incident/accident.

The tramping trip in 'Such a Stupid Way to Die' could have had a very different ending if the party had managed the crisis differently. A different end to the story could have been:

> On the way back up the ridge the victim became slower and slower so the party stopped to assess the situation. He was given someone else's woolly hat (they still had their parka hood), his wet clothes were replaced with dry ones and he was given scroggin to eat. The victim was removed to a flattish sheltered area under a huge rock, then placed in a large plastic bag with a warm party member. They were told to stay put while the other two went out for help. They spent an uncomfortable night but were rescued at midday the following day by an SAR team. The party went on the next tramping club outdoor first aid and bush survival course.

Steps 1-4 of the Crisis Resolution Plan (see page 64) are covered in detail in the NZMSC Manual 14 Outdoor First Aid (pages 7-9, 95-111, 115-117) so they will not be covered here.

A particular crisis may require implementation of only one of the steps towards crisis resolution or it may require all five. The strength of the crisis profile image is that it provides a sensible structure to aim for when organising the complicated events which must be part of any successful crisis resolution.

Use the theoretical crisis scenarios in Chapter 7 (pages 79-87) of this manual to practice using the crisis resolution plan.

FOLLOW-UP TO ACCIDENTS AND INCIDENTS

The fifth step in the Crisis Resolution Plan is follow-up. When formulating a follow-up plan consider these questions:

- With the crisis resolved, should the trip continue?
- Are there loose ends which need consideration?
- Have a plan to deal with the media; contact the appropriate authorities, next of kin etc.
- Why did this happen?
- What events led up to the crisis?
- Could the crisis have been prevented?
- What specific points of learning came from the event?
- In retrospect, how might the crisis have been better managed?
- What resources (human, physical, material) were not available for this crisis resolution which might have improved its management?
- Implement recommended changes to future similar activities/crisis.

The word crisis in this list of questions may well be substituted for 'incident', and the follow-up plan implemented after **all** accidents or near misses. The **Accident Ratio Study** (fig. 2, page 4)[4] clearly indicates how foolish it would be to investigate only the relatively few events where serious or disabling injury occurred when there are many other incidents which could be followed-up. These need to be looked at critically to determine their potential for a more serious accident. (Remember, stubbed toes probably don't require further investigation but stove incidents probably do).

Any organisation wanting to prevent injuries, and to reduce loss and damage, should consider examining the total pattern of accidental happenings, whether or not injury or property damage has occurred.

The following section offers ways of doing this.

THE CAUSAL SEQUENCE—PATHWAYS TO CHANGE

Another analogy which is far more sophisticated than the slot machine and the lemons is: **Pathways to Change**.

This analogy goes a step further than spotting lemons. It helps us identify where the **real** cause of the accident lies, allowing us to find pathways to block or changes to make in the web of events leading to an accident to reduce the chances of it happening again.

Domino Sequence

H.W. Heinrich[5] was a pioneer in safety management, and his original domino sequence was a classic in safety thinking and teaching for over thirty years in many different countries. It showed that all accidents could be traced back to 'the fault of a person' who was genetically or socially impaired. Safety management was simply a matter of inspecting for 'unsafe acts'—establishing **blame** on a person, and engineering 'safe equipment' so accidents couldn't happen. Research data has since shown that these methods have not reduced accident rates, and thinking has moved on since then.[6]

Germaine & Bird[7] took Heinrich's domino sequence further to show three levels of causes of accidents:

— Immediate causes.
— Basic causes.
— Lack of management control factors.

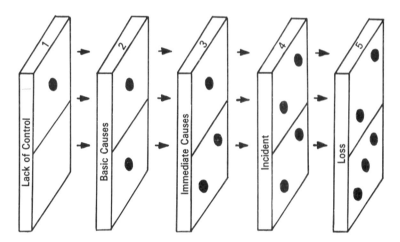

Fig. 28: Domino Sequence (Bird and Germaine 1987)

They also eliminated the false illusion that removing one of the dominoes in the sequence will prevent an accident. On the contrary they revealed that the causes of accidents are complex and occur at different levels. This model traces all accidents back to a lack of management control. Identifying the levels can identify opportunities for intervention.

Pathways to Change

This model (like the Domino Sequence) traces all accidents back to a lack of management control. It assumes that all employees are doing their best to keep themselves and their groups safe in the environment in which they work. There is therefore **no** blame to attribute but rather a need to look at management systems and practices to ensure accidents don't happen.

The following model, a five stage causal sequence, is a combination of the Domino Sequence and the Causal Sequence Model. It elaborates on the simplified causal sequence (Chapter 3, page 19) by showing not only the events leading up to the loss but by identifying pathways between each, where changes can be made, or events blocked.

As a result, the complexity of events leading to accidents or incidents can, in one way, be viewed quite positively ... it shows there are many **pathways** to intervene in or interrupt the sequence to ultimately reduce the chances of a similar incident happening again. Current work in this field has established that the causes of accidents are not linear as the following examples (see figs. 30 & 31) suggest. They are multi-linear and more web-like than sequential. For more information about accident webs and fault trees which stem from the concepts of the basic models discussed here, see further reading page 104.

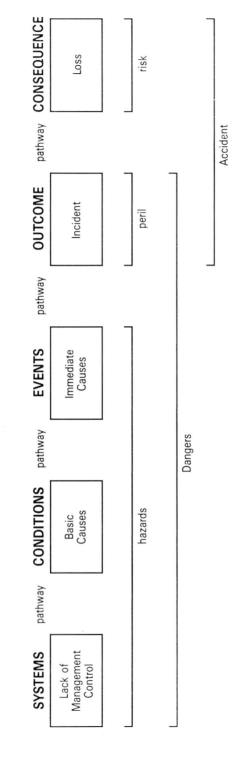

Fig. 29: The Causal Sequence — pathways to change
(Adapted from Kates, Hohenemser & Kasperson 1985, Germain & Bird 1987)

Student fall incident

The following incident will be analysed to determine its causes. Strategies will then be identified to rectify the problem areas.

Incident:
Teenager falls backwards from the top of a stair bannister onto the floor below (3 metres).

Sequence of events:
The student is on a camp based at a lodge. There is no comfortable, small meeting area for co-ed students (dorms are out of bounds to opposite sex) so students have a habit of congregating on the carpeted stairs between the two dormitories. One student was sitting on the bannister. As she went to jump off, she overbalanced and fell backwards, landing on the floor 3 metres below. She got a real shock, and a few bruises, staff were stressed with dealing with it and dinner was delayed as a result.

This accident had the potential for serious injury, a full investigation was required. The following Incident Analysis Form (fig. 30) is an excellent tool to assist with such investigations. It helps determine the root causes of this accident. Fig. 31 identifies the pathways to change or block events, and lists possible ways of doing so at each stage of the causal sequence. Obviously the earlier the changes are put in place (i.e. at the management control level) the better the outcome.

INCIDENT ANALYSIS FORM

LACK OF CONTROL	BASIC CAUSES	IMMEDIATE CAUSES	INCIDENT	LOSS
Inadequate Programme •Failure to recognise need for suitable small area in lodge where teenagers could safely meet to talk	**Personal Factors** •Time—predinner, everyone tired from the day's activities i.e. stress.	**Substandard Practices** •Sitting in an unsafe place. •Poor balance when getting off.	Student falls 3m backwards off stair bannister between lodge dorms.	**People** •Student shocked and upset. •Some bruising to back and limbs. •Stress on staff to deal with it. **Property** •None **Process** •Student needs to take it easy for few days. •Dinner delayed.
Inadequate Standards Inadequate compliance with standards.	**Job Factors** •Inadequate area for co-ed teenagers to gather to talk in the lodge. •Inadequate supervision.	**Substandard Conditions** •Bannister slopes downwards—it is an unsafe place to sit. •3m drop to floor.		

HAZARDS

DANGERS

PERIL

RISK

ACCIDENT

Fig. 30: Incident analysis form—student fall incident (Adapted from Loss Control Management Systems Bird and Germaine 1987)

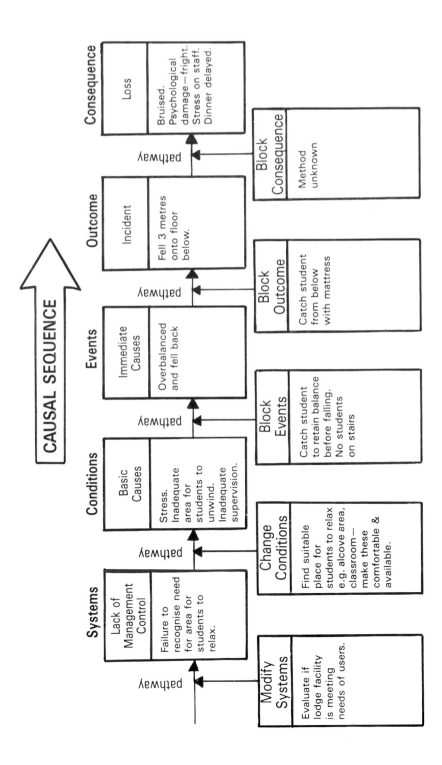

Fig. 31: Pathways to change and/or block events — student fall incident
(Adapted from Kates, Hohenemser & Kasperson 1985, Bird and Germaine 1987)

71

Once a thorough investigation has taken place to determine the root causes of the accident, steps must be taken to remedy this situation if possible. This is the *follow-up* stage.

FOLLOW-UP ACTION TO FALL INCIDENT:

Recommendations:

Find suitable space in lodge for co-ed students to gather.

Option 1. Consider finding alternative space to store tables and chairs which are stored in small annex room which is carpeted, so this area could be utilised for above purpose.
Have new area for storage of tables built.

Option 2. Consider getting carpet for classroom (attached to lodge) to create similar area. Make classroom available to be used in the evenings (locked at present).

Note: Accidents do not only happen out of doors during programmed outdoor activities such as camps. Perhaps this is an area where our *'guard is dropped'* as leaders.

Accident/incident investigation and reporting processes

Crucial to the implementation of an effective risk management programme, is to acknowledge and discuss all accidents and near misses and learn from them. This means:
— disassociating responsibility from blame
— making the process as simple as possible
— making the process non-threatening.

There are several effective ways of doing this.

Debriefing

At the end of an outdoor activity, camp or excursion, get together all staff and helpers involved (and in some cases the participants) for feedback. One format for debriefing a camp is as follows. A simple agenda of three topics:

1. Incidents/accidents which have occurred and strategies for their future avoidance.

2. Week as a whole: suggestions for improvement.

3. Week as a whole: things which worked well.

During the informal discussion of incidents, information can be gathered and recorded by a volunteer scribe on the sequence of events leading to each incident (which could even go back several weeks). Identifying the 'lemons' and seeing where they come in the causal sequence can then be discussed or analysed later. Finally, suggestions for blocking the pathways to prevent the event recurring should be discussed.

Follow-up involves implementing these ideas which could result in minor and/or major changes to the programme in future.

Notable incidents and serious accidents

These should be discussed and a report written as soon as possible after the event. (These reports should be filed together). There are a number of suitable standard forms around which could be adapted to an organisation's own needs, or used as they are. Samples are as follows:

1. Project Adventure New Zealand Accident Report Form (see fig. 32).

2. Incident Analysis Form—adapted from LCMS incident analysis form (see fig. 33).

3. Pathways to change and/or block events—blank form (see fig. 34).

4. Minimum data set for injury surveillance (see fig. 35).

Gathering data on incidents and accidents can be useful for several purposes:

(a) A medium for acknowledging incidents and accidents so people can learn from them.

(b) A record of the event to go to appropriate authorities.

(c) A record of the types of 'incidents' which happen to see if any patterns or common types emerge. These can then be given special attention.

(d) A tool for organising your thoughts afterwards, to understand how the incident happened.

(e) A tool for planning clear strategies for accident prevention in the future.

(f) A tool which will lead to even higher quality experiences in the outdoors.

If these records are pooled they can provide a database from which better quality decisions/programmes can evolve and hence outdoor educators can learn from other peoples experiences as well as their own.

73

SAMPLE ACCIDENT REPORT FORMS

The following **sample accident report forms** (Figs. 32-35) may be useful starting points to adapt to your organisation's needs.

Project Adventure, Inc.
NEW ZEALAND
AOTEAROA

ACCIDENT REPORT FORM

WORKSHOP: _____ WORKSHOP DATES: _____

FACILITATORS: _____ LOCATION: _____

NO. OF HOURS: _____ NO. OF PARTICIPANTS: _____

TOTAL PARTICIPANT HRS: _____

1.A Injury ☐ Illness ☐ Incident ☐ (Describe) _____
      (near miss)   (Choose from Part II)

Date: _____ Activity: _____ Time: _____
                          (Choose from Part II)

Geographic Location: _____

1.B Name of Participant: _____

Address: _____

Med. Evacuation : No/Yes METHOD: _____

Result: _____

Pre-existing Condition? No/Yes
Indicated on Health Release form No/Yes

1.C Weather Temp _____ Precipitation _____ Visibility _____
      Clouds _____ Winds _____

2.A Type of Injury/Illness (May be duplicated from Part I)

☐ Abrasion   ☐ Frostbite   ☐ Fracture   ☐ Hyperthermia
☐ Burn   ☐ Fatigue   ☐ Sprain   ☐ Hypothermia
☐ Concussion ☐ Laceration   ☐ Strain   ☐ Infection
☐ Contusion   ☐ Puncture   ☐ Allergy   ☐ Asthma

☐ Other: _____

2.B Programme Activity

☐ Travel to/from activity   ☐ Mohawk Walk   ☐ Seagull
☐ Games (Specify)   ☐ Nitro crossing   ☐ Disc Jockey
☐ Initiative (Specify)   ☐ Spider's Web   ☐ Bosun's Bridge
☐ Spotting   ☐ Swinging Log   ☐ Cat Walk
☐ Abseil   ☐ Swinging Tyres   ☐ Dangle Duo
☐ Buildering   ☐ TP Shuffle   ☐ Vertical Plunge
☐ Climbing Wall   ☐ Tension Traverse ☐ Heebie Jeebie
☐ All Aboard   ☐ Trolley   ☐ Inclined Log
☐ Trust Fall (Specify)   ☐ Vertical Pole   ☐ Multivine
☐ Beams   ☐ Wall   ☐ Pamper Plank
☐ Bosun's Chair   ☐ Wild Woosey   ☐ Pamper Pole
☐ Criss Crotch   ☐ Chicken Wire   ☐ Tired 2 Line
☐ Fidget Ladder   ☐ 2 Line Bridge
☐ Hickory Jump   ☐ Flying Squirrel
☐ Hole in One   ☐ Zip Wire
☐ Maze

Specify: _____ Other: _____

3. Contributing factors or Type or Near Miss/Incident (You can tick more than one):

☐ Caught in/on/between   ☐ Struck By   ☐ Slip/fall/level different
☐ Clothing   ☐ Fatigue   ☐ Slip/fall/same level
☐ Darkness   ☐ Participant Action   ☐ Speed
☐ Drugs/alcohol   ☐ Lightning   ☐ Instruction
☐ Equipment   ☐ Medication   ☐ Supervision
☐ Exceed Abilities   ☐ Missing/lost   ☐ Unbelayed
☐ Instructions not Followed ☐ Protection failure   ☐ Unfit student
☐ Falling rock/object   ☐ Psychological   ☐ Weather
☐ Striking against

Other: _____

NARRATIVE:

(Describe how the accident happened, Include medical treatment given, and deposition of victim)

_____
_____
_____
_____
_____

Fig. 32(a): Project Adventure accident report form

PROJECT ADVENTURE NEW ZEALAND
PATIENT REPORT FORM

DETAILS

PATIENTS NAME: | Ref. No.
ADDRESS: | Age | Sex:
Location of Incident:
Known Medical Conditions: | Date: | Time:

TIMES				
Pulse				
Blood Pressure				
Respirations				

ASSESSMENT

LEVELS OF CONSCIOUSNESS
Conscious and Co-operative ....
Conscious and Confused ....
Unconscious - Responds to Voice ....
Unconscious - Responds to Pain ....
Unconscious - No Response ....

PUPILS	L	R	L	R	L	R
Reactive						
Fixed						
Dilated						
Pinpoint						

SKIN COLOUR
Normal
Pallid
Flushed
Cyanosed

Diagram Observations
(location of Injury)
A = abrasion
B = burn
C = cut
F = fracture
L = laceration
P = pain
S = swelling

Respirations
normal
shallow
deep
ABSENT

Pulse
full
weak
irregular
ABSENT

HISTORY   Was the Patient Unconscious   Yes/No   How Long For?
Chief Complaint

COMMENTS:

TREATMENT

PROVISIONAL DIAGNOSIS
TREATMENT GIVEN

Medical Assistance
Scene ☐   Dr.
Name

MEDICATION
Time   Dose

Signed: Name

ANALYSIS:
(Include any recommendations, suggestions and observations).

FACILITATORS:
(Comments, recommendations, programme changes).

Possible contact Patient Bodily Fluids   ☐ YES   ☐ NO

TYPE:

Facilitators Signature   Date

INCIDENT ANALYSIS FORM

LACK OF CONTROL	BASIC CAUSES	IMMEDIATE CAUSES	INCIDENT	LOSS
Inadequate Programme	Personal Factors	Substandard Practices		People
Inadequate Standards				Property
	Job Factors	Substandard Conditions		
Inadequate compliance with standards				Process

Fig. 33: Incident Analysis form (Adapted from LCMS incident analysis form)

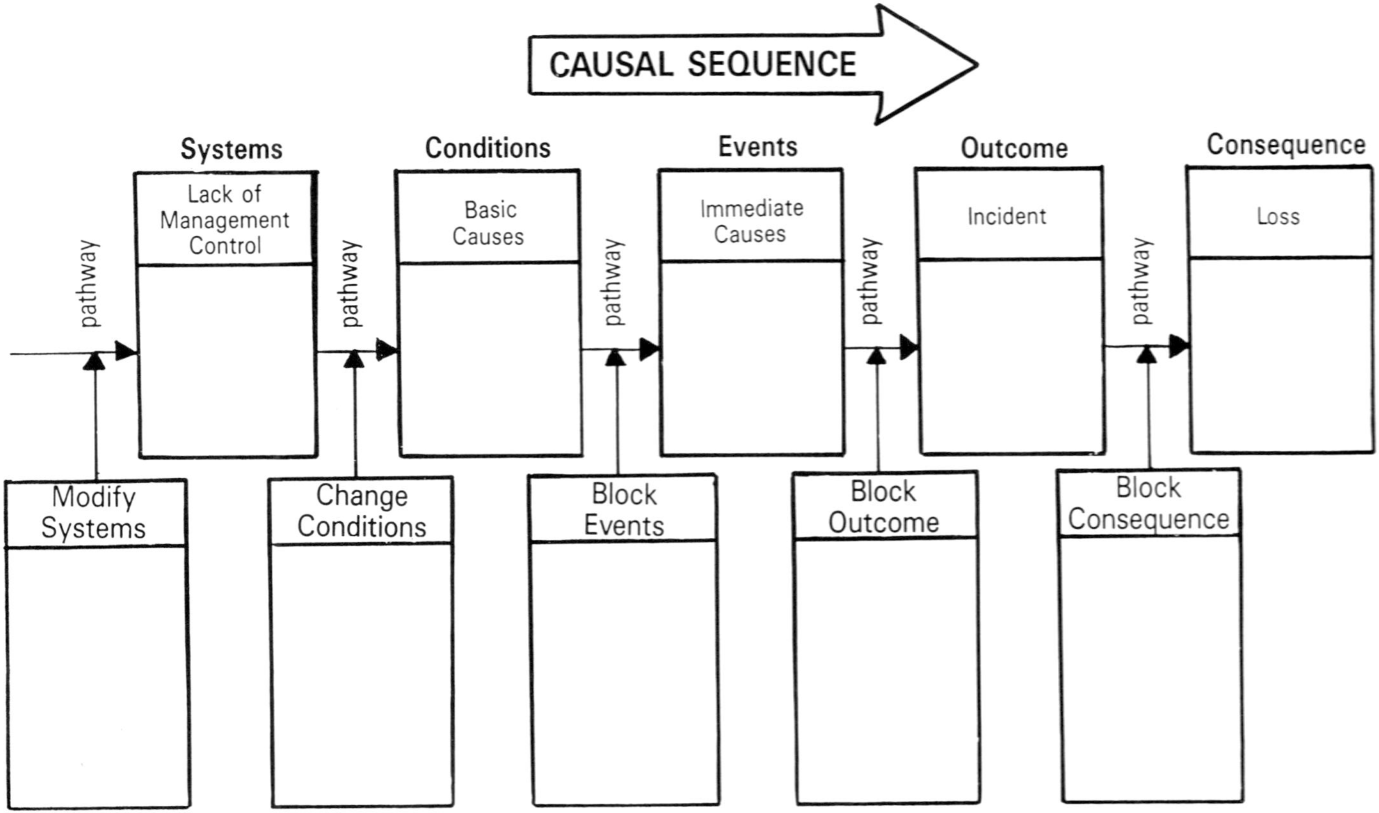

Fig. 34: Pathways to change and/or block events—blank form

77

The following is a list of minimum data for injury surveillance put together by representatives of various bodies who will be required to collect such data in future e.g. hospitals, General Practitioners, Search and Rescue personnel. It may be of use to those groups who wish to design their own forms.

MINIMUM DATA SET FOR INJURY SURVEILLANCE
(as decided at the Consensus Forum, Wellington, 18th March 1992)

DEMOGRAPHIC

Registration date & time
Surname and Forenames
Gender
Date of Birth
Address
Occupation / employment status
Ethnicity

NATURE OF INJURY

Principal injury diagnosis
(Severity [threat to life]—to be a contingent variable, as a derivative of Principal injury diagnosis)

CIRCUMSTANCES OF INJURY

Date of injury occurrence
Time of injury occurrence
Activity
Place of occurrence
Mechanism / External Cause of injury

(Intent—to be a contingent variable, as a derivative of Mechanism/External cause of injury)

Product

(Narrative—not included in National Minimum Data Set, but would be included in regional data).

Fig. 35: Minimum data set for injury surveillance

In New Zealand an accident/incident database is run by the Outdoor Safety Institute, Box 5250, Wellington.

There are also current initiatives happening in New Zealand which are linked into the Injury Prevention Research Unit and the Accident Rehabilitation Compensation and Insurance Corporation. The minimum data set for injury surveillance comes from these initiatives. Contact NZMSC for more information.

CHAPTER 7

CASE STUDIES
Ways to practice applying risk management principles

PLANNING EXERCISES

Twelve planning exercises follow.

Each consists of:

(i) An activity with a description of the type of people and environment involved.

(ii) An incident which could occur while the activity is underway.

For each activity:

(a) List some of the risks and management techniques involved when planning the activity, using the RAMS form.

(b) Decide how you would deal with the incident and how you would prevent it happening again.

Activity

1. NIGHTLINE

A sensory walk (blindfolded) outside the training centre, through bush.

Twenty-five 15 year old students, two teachers.

2. CONFIDENCE COURSE

A confidence course in a bush environment, afternoon session, cold overcast day.

Twenty 4th formers, resident teacher, one NZMSC instructor, two 7th form helpers.

3. BUSHCRAFT COURSE

A weekend Bushcraft Course for physically disabled young adults.

Ten participants, two in wheelchairs, three NZMSC Bushcraft Instructors.

4. SKIING

A day trip to the snow for $35 \times$ 4th Formers.

One asthmatic child, one deaf child, two teachers, three parents.

5. RIVER CROSSING

A half day river crossing exercise in a South Island braided river in November, overcast, cold.

Fifteen $\times$ Outdoor Education teachers
Three $\times$ NZMSC instructors.

6. COMPASS WORK

Having taught a group of ten ranger guides the basics of using a compass to find and follow a bearing, you now set a practical exercise for them to practice this skill.

Beech forest environment, winter, cold but fine.

1. NIGHTLINE INCIDENT

Two students sneak away from the group and hide in the bush. The teachers don't realise this until they return to the lodge and are told by other students. Thirty minutes have passed and there is still no sign of the students.

2. CONFIDENCE COURSE INCIDENT

One student gets half way along the three wire bridge and freezes where the wires are their slackest.

3. BUSHCRAFT COURSE INCIDENT

While travelling through bushed area, the people in front disturb a wasp nest. One person is stung on the head five times. Two or three others are also stung.

4. SKIING INCIDENT

At the end of the day the deaf child has not assembled at the meeting place.

5. RIVERCROSSING INCIDENT

One person panics while practising the linked arm and pole method in thigh deep swift water. They lose their grip and start screaming. (You later discover this person has previously had a bad river crossing experience).

6. COMPASS WORK INCIDENT

Ten minutes after the specified return to base time, two girls have not arrived.

7. EMERGENCY FIRELIGHTING

You are instructing a group of 20 tramping club members in the skill of emergency firelighting. Bush environment, drizzly day. One other instructor and two assistant instructors present.

8. STOVE LIGHTING

You are teaching a group of eight assistant instructors how to light four different types of stoves.

1. Optimus (white spirit stove)
2. Gaz stove (gas stove)
3. MSR whisperlight (white spirit - pressure stove)
4. Trangia (meths-burning stove)

9. FARM PARK VISIT

You are in charge of 15 Standard 4 children visiting a farm park to study the animals.

10. BOTANICAL GARDENS

You are in charge of 18 children visiting the botanical gardens to observe the wonders of spring.

11. FARM VISIT

You are in charge of 24 children visiting a farm.

12. AIRPORT VISIT

You are in charge of 20 preschool children visiting the airport.

7. EMERGENCY FIRELIGHTING INCIDENT

One person finds an ideal dry spot for their fire in the base of a hollow tree and gets a cracking fire going. The tree itself is smouldering when you arrive on the scene.

8. STOVE LIGHTING INCIDENT

One person overpumps the MSR stove and it flares up, singeing their eyebrows and giving them a real fright.

9. FARM PARK VISIT INCIDENT

One child gets too close to the fish pond, slips and falls in.

10. BOTANICAL GARDENS INCIDENT

Two children wander off and become lost.

11. FARM VISIT INCIDENT

Two children start teasing a dog chained up to a fencepost and one child is finally bitten by the dog.

12. AIRPORT VISIT INCIDENT

Two pupils sit on the baggage escalator and one gets carried through the flaps into the baggage handling area. They are screaming because they can't get off.

CRISIS MANAGEMENT EXERCISES

Three crisis scenarios follow.

Complete the following exercises as suggested.

INCIDENT A

You have had a five day tent/camp with your class of 13-14 year olds at the bushline in a Canterbury valley, to study vegetation change with altitude, aspect and rain-shadow effects. The valley is part of a tramping route over an easy Main Divide Pass.

The tent/camp is two hours walk up valley from the road-end where you left the school bus. (It is 11km from there out to the main road).

Part of the original plan (approved by the Principal, Board of Trustees, and parents) was that, subject to the weather and other factors, you would take a group of up to eight students (who have proved fit and capable in the five day tent based section) on a two day tramp over the pass. You know the route personally. It is decided to take seven students (of whom two are girls) and one other fit experienced teacher.

The other four adults will return to the bus with the rest of the class (well led by their last year's teacher).

You had intended the other adult with you to be one of the women teachers but by lunchtime on Day 5 she has a very sore throat and feels seedy so asks to be replaced by a male teacher. In view of this, you and she consider not letting the girls go on your trip, but there are howls of protest from everyone so you take the girls.

Day 5: After an early evening meal your small group move on up-valley to a hut, 1½ hours walk away. You have decided to use the hut to save weight. By moving up-valley this evening you shorten the next day's trip over the pass. It also puts you up-valley of the only questionable river crossing (it is a confined river and rises quickly during rain) which is just below the hut. (The only mandatory river-crossing on Day 6 is the West Coast river which has a forestry bridge).

Day 6: Tent/camp group break camp, walk back to bus, cross Main Divide by road, and set up camp again at the mouth of the West Coast Valley you will come down.

Your party is to cross the pass today and descend to a hut half-way down the valley. The intention for Day 7 is that as your group tramps on down to the road (four hour walk), the tent/group will come up-valley on a day walk to study vegetation and meet you en route, descending with you to the bus, then home.

Both parties have radios. You plan a 6.00 pm schedule each day.

Your estimated times for Day 6 are two hours to the pass and three more to the hut. There are mares' tails in the sky and a weird light in the morning, but the radio forecast the previous night was for settled weather the next day, possibly north-westerly on Day 7.

It takes you 3½ hours to reach the pass. The ground is much more boggy than you remember, one boy has complained of sore heels (but said he didn't want to put plasters on) and one girl is uncharacteristically pale and slow.

You had planned to have lunch down at the creek on the West Coast side of the pass but it is already noon when you reach the summit. At this rate you guess it will take 4½ hours to reach the hut.

At this point one boy discovers he has left his asthma inhaler (ventilator) under the mattress in the last hut and the boy with sore heels now has blisters which need tending, they are huge and broken. The pale girl looks ill but insists she is okay. Her pack is light and her feet are in good shape. You suspect menstrual disorders but with two male adults she won't say.

The route down the pass is over steep tussock slopes to the river from where a good track leads through the impenetrable scrub masking big boulders. The entrance to the track, however is hard to pick up unless you know where it is. You are the only one who does.

In spite of the forecast, wind and cloud have increased rapidly all morning and the north-westerly rain is just starting. You take out the radio to try a 'sked', only to find that whoever dismantled the aerial last night broke off one of the input plugs and you can get no reception at all.[1]

Clearly a decision is required.

(i)   List the **causal factors** which led to this crisis.
(ii) Decide on an **action plan** to deal with this situation.
(iii) Fill out a Pathways to Change form (fig. 35) identifying the pathways to change or block events.
(iv) List the changes which need to be made to avoid a future recurrence of such an incident i.e. **a follow-up plan**.

INCIDENT B

An organised trip in Canadian Canoes down the Wanganui River in April (autumn). The group consists of ten women aged 30-60. They have two instructors in kayaks.

All arrive at the meeting point. The two instructors are a little late and under the weather after a late night out the night before. They don't have much prior knowledge of how experienced the group is. The group is told how to handle the boats while on the bank (not in them) and are also told they don't need kneepads. The only chance they have to practise is in a side stream while waiting for speedboats to go by.

At the first rapid the instructors paddle down and wait. All five Canadians capsize in the rapid. Incorrect position (i.e. sitting), meant the paddlers had no means of bracing when the boats became unstable so they went over.

One person was stuck under a boat for some time. She kept hold of her paddle while her partner let hers go. Luckily the boat was upside down in deep water so she could push herself down to get out. However, she also got caught in the webbing which was holding the gear in the boat. The women could not turn the boat over by themselves. The one who got stuck had difficulty breathing and a constricted throat (shock/relief?) once she was free. It took some time to calm her.

All paddlers got wet in the first rapid. They are now very worried about the rest of the trip, however they have had prior experience working together as a group in the outdoors.

Clearly some things need to be sorted out before this trip continues.

(i) List the **causal factors** which led to this crisis.
(ii) Decide on an **action plan** to deal with this situation.
(iii) Fill out a Pathways to Change form (fig. 35) identifying the pathways to change or block events.
(iv) List the changes which need to be made to prevent a future recurrence of such an incident, i.e. **follow-up plan**.

INCIDENT C

Seven 6th form students, a parent and the teacher from a country school visit Christchurch city for their annual city field trip. They travel 400kms in two cars (adults driving) to arrive in the city just on dark, with everyone more than ready for a meal. They have trouble finding a suitable cafe with adequate parking so frustrations run high. The two cars are separated, so each group finds food separately and makes their way independently to their cabin accommodation. They plan the next day's excursions, and go to bed after some card playing and cups of tea.

The students' assignment involves navigating their way around a planned route of the city (in pairs or threes) by bus; making phonecalls using phonecards and locating points of interest such as QE11 Park. They are dropped off in Cathedral Square at 9.30 am and are told they will be picked up there at 4 pm.

All students have been gone for two hours. The teacher and parent are cosily ensconced in a cafe, drinking tea and listening to the piped radio music. During the newsbreak they hear there is a bus strike that afternoon to begin at midday. It is 11.40 am. They have made no alternative arrangements should something like this occur!

What would you do?

(i)   List the **causal factors** which led to this crisis.
(ii) Decide on an **action plan** to deal with this situation.
(iii) Fill out a Pathways to Change form (fig. 35) identifying the pathways to change or block events.
(iv) List the changes which need to be made to prevent a future recurrence of such an accident, i.e. **follow-up plan**.

Appendix A

REASONS FOR RISK MANAGEMENT

LEGAL AND MORAL RESPONSIBILITIES

A person with responsibility for others in the outdoors, has a moral obligation to provide them with a safe, enjoyable experience due to a high degree of care. Both society and the participants would expect this.

Duty of care owed

Legally, people who take on responsibility for others in the outdoors, are subject to civil and criminal liability under the Crimes Act 1961 and the Children and Young Persons Act 1974. Under this legislation, The Duty of Care owed to students who are minors is that of 'In Loco Parentis'. This doctrine requires the person(s) responsible for the minor to give them the degree of care attributable to a reasonably careful and prudent parent. The Duty of Care owed to adult students is also governed by civil and criminal legislation and by **sound common practice**. While the nature of the care required will differ from that owed to minors, the standard will not.

Standard of care owed

It must be stressed that juries in the past have set the standard of care required at a very high level.

More information regarding the legal responsibilities of Principals, Boards of Trustees and Teachers may be found in the Department of Education Circulars: 1985/1 and 1988/28, though these are being revised.

Code of Practice

A Code of Practice for Education Outside the Classroom is currently being developed to guide boards of trustees, principals and teachers through the various implications of legislation changes, and to advise on appropriate guidelines for the policies for EOTC programmes.

In particular, the code is expected to cover:

- legal liabilities and responsibilities of the board of trustees, principal and the teachers;
- policies needed to cover procedures, standards;
- supervision of EOTC programmes;
- staffing for EOTC activities, in the context of the whole health and safety programme;
- training for staff—teachers, parent helpers;
- insurance requirements.

The Code of Practice should provide valuable guidance towards effective safety management in EOTC.[1]

Changes to legislation

During 1992/3 substantial changes to the relevant legislation affecting outdoor educators have occurred. They include such areas of legislation as the:

- Health and Safety in Employment Act 1992
- Employment Contracts Act
- Industry Training Act 1992
- Accident Compensation Insurance.

These changes sharpen the overall move towards 'quality systems', and clearly focus the demand for increasing **professionalism** and appropriate **standards of performance** from both individual providers and controlling organisations.

Four main parts to new laws

Four main parts to the new legislation, in their different ways, are likely to impinge on the way schools will write their policies for EOTC and run their programmes:

• Health and Safety in Employment Act 1992.

This Act, which became law on April 1, 1993, covers all the issues of safety and health at places of work, but the full details of the regulations are not yet available. The two fundamental objects are to prevent harm to employees at work; and to ensure actions 'at work' do not result in harm to other people, including members of the public.

Clearly, this could have important implications for the protection of students.

The Act promotes standards of excellence in health and safety management, and requires people in places of work to perform specific duties to ensure that no-one is harmed as a result of work activities. It also provides for the making of regulations and approved codes of practice relating to specific hazards.

• Employment Contracts Act

This act makes provision for the specification of the duties carried out 'at work,' and enables employers to involve employees in the whole process of safety management — identification of potential hazards; elimination, isolation or minimisation of hazards; training and qualification of employees to work safely; appropriate supervision and experience; development of policies for safety and health.

• Industry Training Act 1992

This Act has enabled the establishment of industry training organisations, and provides a framework for 'industry' to take control of the development implementation and administration of its own industry training programmes.

Training can then be designed for industry by the industry, and can be integrated into the New Zealand Qualification Authority's national qualifications framework at the appropriate levels and standards.

In terms of the 'outdoor industry,' two initiatives have taken place. The Hillary Commission has acted in the formation of a Sport, Fitness and Leisure Industry Training Organisation (SFLITO), which includes outdoor recreation under its umbrella of activities. At the same time, the professional adventure tourism sector is linking its training needs with other sectors of the tourism industry, under the Aviation, Tourism & Travel Training Organisation.

Ultimately, it is to be hoped these initiatives will arrive at appropriate training systems to meet the needs of both the outdoor recreationists, and the adventure industry, with presumably the common point being at the standards required by NZQA.

Systems and standards of training for outdoor leaders are a critical area for the safety of EOTC programmes.

• Accident compensation insurance

Implications in the changes to the ACC system will need to be considered by schools drawing up their policies for EOTC.

For example, the limits for compensation for the costs of taking a pupil to hospital after an accident may have implications for the school's insurance cover. There may be other areas where parents might seek redress from the school through the courts.[2]

EMPLOYERS' RESPONSIBILITIES

The employer or controlling authority has ultimate responsibility for approval of outdoor programmes, so the 'buck' ultimately rests with them.

The following questions need to be asked:

Employee: Are there rules laid out by my employer?
Am I operating within them?

Employer: Are there clearly defined standards for this programme?
Are the staff operating within these?

ADMINISTRATOR'S RESPONSIBILITIES

An administrator with responsibility for outdoor programmes (e.g. Teacher in Charge of Education Outside the Classroom (EOTC), Principal, Board of Trustees member) is usually removed from the 'action' so to speak, yet has responsibility for approval of the programme, and is probably accountable if something goes wrong.

There are two tools which can help you to make informed decisions when approving programmes, improve support for programmes and staff, and improve accountability between administrators and outdoor leaders.

The first is the RAMS or plan (see page 39). A copy of this document could easily be part of the required paperwork for programme approval.

The second is a list of:

Thirty questions administrators should ask about their outdoor education programmes.[3]

STAFF:

1. Are appropriate personnel employed? (for the participants and for the programme?).

2. Are staff trained in the activities they will teach in first aid, and in risk management?

3. Is there provision for ongoing staff training?
   —In technical skills (are staff up-to-date)?
   —In people skills (learning development, group management, debriefing skills)
   —In first aid?
   —In risk management?

4. Are staff familiar with the type of terrain to be used?

5. Is there a procedure for inducting new staff to the programme?

PROGRAMME:

6. Has the programme a written objective?

7. Are the risks in the programme essential to the objective?

8. Will the programme be likely to discourage any participants from further use of the outdoors?

9. Is there a progression of activities and a sequential learning plan?

10. Do you, as administrator, have a general understanding of the nature of the programme and the nature of the terrain used?

11. Is participation voluntary?

12. Is there a route plan for trips, including a copy for you?

13. Does the programme indicate there will be minimal environmental impact?

14. Is there scope for alterations to the programme as experience indicates the need? (Do these alterations need to be authorised by you?)

EVALUATION:

15. Is there provision for regular evaluation of the programme?

    (a) Staff meetings? Briefing, Debriefing?
    (b) Annual overall evaluation?
    (c) Accident and 'near miss' records?
    (d) Ongoing briefing and debriefing with participants?

16. Are you able to attend staff meetings?

17. Does the programme call for evaluation by the participants?

PARTICIPANTS:

18. Are the participants (and their parents in the case of minors) informed of the nature of the programme and of the terrain?

19. Have the students (and their parents) been questioned about their medical history?

20. Have the students been screened and their capacity considered against the programme?

EQUIPMENT:

21. Is the appropriate equipment available?

22. Is responsibility for pools of equipment and facilities designated individual staff?

23. Are there procedures for maintaining equipment and facilities?

LOGISTICS:

24. Are there potential transportation problems? (e.g. dense traffic times, overtired drivers, poorly maintained vehicles).

25. In the case of minors is their written parental consent on file?

26. Have you the necessary information to contact next of kin?

27. Has the need to gain permission to use the terrain been considered?

28. Has the need to leave notice of intentions with land/sea managers been considered?

FRAMEWORK:

29. Is there an operational framework? (accepted procedures; ratio of staff to participants; agreed areas of operation).

30. Is there provision for emergencies? (communication, transport, first aid facilities, shelter).

If, as an administrator with responsibility for an outdoor programme, you are unable to answer 'yes' to the above questions, then you need to consider one or a combination of the following:

— Seek further information from the leader or instructor.
— Allocate further resources to the programme.
— Seek advice from an outside agency.
— Alter or cancel the programme.

PROFESSIONALISM

Sound professional practice vs common practice

Sound professional practice is safe practice in accordance with a profession's stated standards. **Common practice** is that which is commonly used and accepted by members of a profession. When the two are not in accordance with one another, as sometimes happens in various professional fields, for example law or medicine, problems can arise. The outdoor adventure field is no different.

(A) An outdoor instructor gave the 'minimum impact' talk to a group of students on the first day of their four day camp. Over the next four days the instructor was observed to do the following:

- cover the unsightly fireplace with a single rock after a firelighting exercise when all had been asked to leave the site as they found it
- weed their campsite of 15 or so small native plants before pitching their tent

(B) An abseiling instructor abseiled down a rockface at the end of the day, McGyver style, narrowly missing hitting three people below. They did this:

- without a safety rope or belayer
- without checking that it was clear below (the rock overhung, and the previous abseiler was still being assisted out of the harness by two instructors).

Luckily a third person, standing further back from the rockface shouted: 'Get outa the way!' just in time for all three people below to stand clear, as they could not see the abseiler descending. The instructor said, 'I always finish my sessions in this way and have never hurt anyone yet'.

(C) An outdoor education teacher led a group of fourth form students on a three day expedition into an alpine environment, in winter. On the second day a changeover of support staff was required and an arrangement was made for this to take place. Due to deteriorating weather and snow overnight, two staff went to the rendezvous point to ensure extra support if required. On arrival at the rendezvous point, the group was not there so it was assumed they must still be at the alpine hut. The two staff continued to climb to the hut in deteriorating conditions—heavy snow, strong winds. The hut was empty on arrival, and in the hut intentions book, in a student's handwriting was written: 'Gone back to base'. As the two staff had not met the group on their way up to the hut, it was assumed the group had taken the more exposed, ridge track back to base camp, so they decided to follow in case assistance was required. Part way along the ridge, conditions became so difficult that they felt they were putting themselves in danger so they retraced their steps to the hut and back to base camp. This excursion took from 9 am until 4 pm. On arrival back at base camp, they were alarmed to find the group had not yet returned, and it was getting dark (darkness 5.30 pm). It was decided to check all escape routes.

Two parties were despatched with radios, one to check the alternative route down from the alpine hut from the opposite end, the other to check the low level hut which was to be the original destination for the group on the second night.

The party were found happily settled in the second hut oblivious to all the worry which had been caused. When asked about the intentions written in the alpine hut book, the leader said he 'didn't know who had written it or why', and that he 'never wrote in hut books, as didn't see any need'.

On the matter of the missed rendezvous, the leader said, 'We were a bit early, and were having no problems, so decided to just keep going'.

Clearly these are examples of **common practice** for the instructors concerned and perhaps some of their peers. It is equally clear that the behaviour described does not denote **sound professional practice**. Indeed, they resulted in a degree of harm to people, to the environment or to process (interruption to the activity or programme concerned).

A report by the National Safety Network[4] in the United States, indicates that staff injury rates in outdoor activities have actually been higher than student rates in three of four years of data collection. The computation was based on the number of injuries divided by the number of staff days. (The cumulative student rate was .00029 as compared to a staff injury rate of .00032). Why do staff get injured more often than students? Is it increased exposure to risk, inherent to the job, or increased carelessness, inherent to the attitude?[5]

Some staff members, who are fully aware of these risks, like to operate on the edge. These people can be a liability to themselves, their organisation, and their profession.

Incidents like those described on the previous page reinforce doubts about whether outdoor education is a profession or merely a fun occupation. The difference is in the application of expectations and standards. **Professionalism**, by definition, requires a certain standard of performance which all the instructors in the examples lack. Professionalism is developed as part of belonging and being responsible to a profession.

- Each member of the profession is a link in the organisational chain which is only as good as its weakest link.
- Professionalism is the temper which gives the chain its strength and quality.

In order to function safely and effectively an organisation must establish clear and concise policies and procedures. If the organisation is part of a larger profession, the policies must be consistent with those recognised by the profession as a whole. If we want our students in the outdoors to develop leadership, responsibility, compassion and safe practices, then it must be role-modelled to them at all levels.[6]

NOTES

Chapter 1

[1]	Ewart, Alan	'Managing Fear in the Outdoor Experiential Setting', *The Journal of Experiential Education*, Spring 1989.
[2]	Raffan, James	'Images for Crisis Management', *The Journal for Experiential Education*, Fall 1984.
[3]	Bird & Germaine	*Practical Loss Control Leadership. The Conservation of People, Property, Process and Profits*, Loganville, Georgia, Institute Publishing, 1987.
[4]	ibid	
[5]	ibid	
[6]	Meyer, Dan	'The Management of Risk', *The Journal of Experiential Education*, Fall 1979.
[7]	Bird & Germaine	op cit
[8]	Johnston, Margaret E.	*Peak Experiences: Risk and Hazard in Mountain Recreation in New Zealand*, unpublished PHD Thesis, Department of Geography, University of Canterbury.

Chapter 2

These definitions come from a set of overheads compiled and presented by Grant Davidson at a Risk Management Seminar, Wellington, October 1992. The source material is quoted below.

[1]	Priest, S; Bailey, R.	Justifying the Risk to Others: The Real Razors Edge, *The Journal of Experiential Education*, 1987.
[2]	Csikszentimihayli, Miholyc;	*Beyond Boredom and Anxiety*, San Francisco 1975.
	Maslow, Abraham	*Toward a Psychology of Being*, D. Van Nostrand Co, Princeton, New Jersey, 1962.

97

[3] Priest, S.; Baillie R.   Justifying the Risk to Others: The Real Razor's Edge, *The Journal of Experiential Education*, 1987.

[4] ibid

[5] ibid

[6] ibid

[7] Snider

[8] Bird, F.E;   *Practical Loss Control Leadership. The Conservation*
Germaine, G.R.   *of People, Property, Process and profits*, Loganville, Georgia, Institute Publishing, 1987.

[9] ibid

[10] ibid

[11] Fowler & Fowler   *Pocket Oxford Dictionary*, University Press, Oxford. 1972.

[12] Davidson, G.   Direct quote (verbal). (1992).

[13] Baillie, R.   *'Hazarding the lives of others: How can we justify it?'*. Paper presented at the AEE Conference Moddus C.T. 1986.

[14] Higgins, L.   *1981 Wilderness Schools: Risk Vs Danger*

[15] Meyer, D.   1979 The Management of Risk. *The Journal of Experiential Education*.

[16] Priest, Simon and   Justifying the Risk to Others: The Real Razor's
Baillie, Rusty   Edge. *Journal of Experiential Education 1987*.

[17] Karetu, Professor   This list was prepared especially for this manual by
Timotis.   Professor Karetu, Commissioner, Te Taura Whiri i te Reo Maori (Maori Language Commission) 1993.

[18] For further information regarding Tikanga Maori and managing risks in the outdoors contact: Te Ao Turoa (Aotearoa Maori Outdoor Leaders' Association Inc.) P.O. Box 1005, Hamilton.

Chapter 3

[1] Priest, Simon and   op cit (1987)
Baillie R.

[2] Schoel J., Prouty D.,   *Islands of Healing*, Project Adventure Inc., Hamilton,
Radcliffe, P.   USA 1989.

[3] Ewert, A.   'Managing Fear in the Outdoor Experiential Education Setting', *The Journal of Experiential Education*, Spring 1989.

[4] ibid

[5] Helms, Michael   Factors Affecting Evaluations of Risks & Hazards in Mountaineering. *Journal of Experiential Education*, Fall 1984. Reviewed climbing accidents 1979.

   Williamson, Jed;   Examined 15 years of accident data from adventure
   Meyer, Dan   based programmes 1979.

[6] ibid

[7] Cartwright, D.   Risk Taking by individuals and groups. *Journal of Personality and Social Psychology* Vol. 20. also: Freedman, Carlsmith & Sears, 1970.

[8] Helms, Michael   'Psychological and Sociological Phenomena affecting the perceptions of Risk and Hazard in Mountaineering'. Unpublished manuscript, Evergreen State College, Olympia, Washington, 1982.

[9] Allen, Stewart, D.   *Risk Recreation: A literature Review and Conceptual Model*, unpublished manuscript, School of Forestry, University of Montana, Missoula, 1979.

[10] Freedman, J.L;   *Social Psychology*, Engelwood Cliffs, N.J.: Prentice-
   Carlsmith J.M and   Hall 1970.
   Sears, D. O.

[11] Helms, Michael;   op cit
   Williamson, Jed;
   Meyer Dan

[12] ibid

[13] Baron, Robert A.,   *Social Psychology. Understanding Human
   Byrne Donn   Interaction*, 4th Edition, Alan & Bacon Inc., Boston.

Chapter 4

[1] Pilot Risk Management Training Course held at the Boyle River Lodge in August 1987. Key contributors to designing matris: Ray Goldring, Arthur Sutherland, Bert McConnell.

[2] Davidson, Grant   Adapted from an original paper written in 1987.

Chapter 5

[1] Heron, John   *The self-assessment and peer feedback model.*

[2] All are quotes from evaluations written by Risk Management Course participants, on how they found the John Heron Feedback model.

³ Course information
    For more information contact:
    NZ Mountain Safety Council, Box 6027,
    Te Aro, Wellington. ph (04) 385-7162
    or
    The Hillary Commission
    Box 2251
    Wellington. ph (04) 472-8058

Chapter 6

¹ Raffan, James   'Images for Crisis Management', *The Journal of Experiential Education*, Fall 1984.

² NZMSC   'Such a Stupid way to Die' film/video.

³ Raffan, James   op cit. This section has been adapted from the source material.

⁴ Bird & Germaine   op cit.

⁵ Heinrich, H.W.   *Industrial Accident Prevention: A Scientific Approach* New York: McGraw-Hill Book Co., 1950.

⁶ Davidson, Grant   Risk Management Training Scheme, Course Director's Notes 1993.

⁷ Bird & Germaine   op cit.

Chapter 7

¹ Clark, Margaret   From an original paper.

Appendix A

¹ Trist, Alan   The Safety Issues for Outdoor Education, *Principals Today*, February 1993.

² ibid

³ Allen, Stu   Adapted from 30 Questions Administrators should ask about their Outdoor Education Programmes. *Towards Safety and Environmental Frameworks for New Zealand Outdoor Education in the 1980's*. A Winston Churchill Memorial Trust Fellowship Study, 1983.

⁴ Hale, Alan   National Safety Network International Data Base, Adventure Programmes - Review 1988. *National Safety Network*: Bellefontaine.

⁵ Kolb, David C.   Too Young to Die. *Journal of Experiential Education*, Spring 1989.

⁶ ibid

REFERENCES AND CONTACTS

Accident Compensation Corporation

Individual Responsibility — paper.

Allen, Stewart, D.

Risk Recreation: A literature Review and Conceptual Model, unpublished manuscript, School of Forestry, University of Montana, Missoula, 1979.

Allen, Stu

Towards Safety and Environmental Frameworks for New Zealand Outdoor Education in the 1980's, A Winston Churchill Memorial Trust Fellowship Study, 1983.

Bamford, Dave

Risk Recreation Management in New Zealand, unpublished paper presented at the 1986 Adventure Tourism Seminars, 1986.

Baron, Robert A.
Byrne, Donn

Social Psychology. Understanding Human Interaction, 4th Edition, Alan & Bacon Inc., Boston.

Bird, Frank E. and Germaine, George R.

Practical Loss Control Leadership. The Conservation of People, Property, Process and Profits, Loganville, Georgia, Institute Publishing, 1987.

Blanchard, and Ford, Phyllis

Chapter 8, 'Risk Management', *Leadership and the Administration of Outdoor Pursuits*

Bramfitt, Colin

Notes from Lecture on Risk Management at Little Huia R.M.T.A. Course May 1989.

Button, Ray

Interesting Items. Real Risk or Apparent Risk? Article.

Cartwright, D.

Risk Taking by Individuals and Groups. Journal of Personality and Social Psychology Vol. 20.

Csiksezentmihayli, Miholyc

Beyond Boredom and Anxiety, San Francisco, 1975.

Davidson, Grant

Set of overhead masters, Outdoor Safety Institute, Box 5250, Wellington 1992.

Department of Education

Circular 1985/1. *Education Outside the Classroom: Safety and Supervision*, Wellington, 11 January 1985.

Ibid

Circular 1988/28 *Education Outside the Classroom — Legal Aspects*: Wellington, 13 May 1988.

Ewert, Alan

'Managing Fear in the Outdoor Experiential Education Setting', *The Journal of Experiential Education*, Spring 1989.

Ibid	'The Risk Management Plan: Promises and Pitfalls', *The Journal of Experiential Education*, Fall 1984.
Freedman, J.L. Carlsmith J.M. & Sears D.O.	*Social Psychology*. Engelwood Cliffs, N.J. Prentice-Hall 1970.
Hale, Alan	National Safety Network International Data Base, Adventure Programmes—Review 1988. *National Safety Network*: Bellefontaine.
Hale, Alan	*Safety Management for Outdoor Programme Leaders* Unpublished manuscript 1984.
Heinrich, H.W.	*Industrial Accident Prevention: A Scientific Approach*. New York: McGraw-Hill Book Co. 1950.
Helms, Michael	'Factors Affecting Evaluations of Risks and Hazards in Mountaineering'. *The Journal of Experiential Education*, Fall 1984.
Heron, John	Self and Peer Assessment Model.
Hunt, Jasper S. Jr	'Opinion: The Dangers of Substituting Rules for Instructor Judgement in Adventure programmes'. *Journal of Experiential Education*, Fall 1984.
Johnston, Margaret E.	*Peak Experiences: Risk and Hazard in Mountain Recreation in New Zealand*, unpublished PHD thesis, Department of Geography, University of Canterbury,
Kolb, David C	'Too Young to Die', *The Journal of Experiential Education*, Spring 1989.
Maslow, Abraham	*Toward a Psychology of Being*—D. Van Nostrand Co; Princeton, New Jersey 1962.
Meier, Dr. Joel	A Challenge for the 1980's—Activate and Motivate through Adventure and Risk. A keynote address for the New Zealand A.H.P.E.R. Conference—Auckland, May 15 1980.
Meyer, Dan	'The Management of Risk', *The Journal of Experiential Education*, Fall 1979.
Mobley, Michael	Anatomy of an Accident, *Journal of Experiential Education*, Fall 1984.
NZ Mountain Safety Council	Film/Video: Such a Stupid Way to Die.
NZ Mountain Safety Council	Leadership and Trip Planning, *Bushcraft Manual*, 1987.
NZ Mountain Safety Council	*Outdoor First Aid Manual*, 1984.

NZ Police National
Headquarters

Search and Rescue Operation Reports.

Ogilvie, Ken

The Management of Risk, *Adventure Education*

Open Polytech

Bush Safety and Appreciation *Going Bush*, 1988.

Priest, Simon and
Baillie Rusty

'Justifying the Risk to Others: The Real Razor's Edge',
The Journal of Experiential Education, 1987.

Raffan, James

'Images for Crisis Management', *The Journal for
Experiential Education*, Fall 1984.

Rawson, Gerald et.al

Outdoor Pursuits Guidelines for Educators, Revised
Edition, Wellington, Ministry of Education, May 1990.

Ringer, Martin

'Outdoor Education', February 1985.

Ibid

'Outdoor Leader Training and Assessment. An opinion
on People Skills,' August 1987.

Schoel, J, Prouty, D,
Radcliffe, P.

Islands of Healing, Project Adventure, Inc. Hamilton,
USA 1989.

Stich, Thomas F. and
Gaylor Michael S

'Risk Management in Adventure Programmes with
Special Populations: Two Hidden Dangers', *Journal
of Experiential Education*, Fall 1984.

Trist, Alan

Risk and Responsibility in Outdoor Education,
unpublished paper, NZ Mountain Safety Council,
January 1977.

Trist, Alan

Safety in E.O.T.C., *Parent & School*

Trist, Alan

The Safety Issues for Outdoor Education, *Principals
Today* February 1993.

Warren, Karen

Notes from 'Leadership Styles' workshop.
Christchurch Jan. 1990.

Williamson, Jed

*Accidents in North American Mountaineering: An
Overview*. (Paper presented to the United
International Alpinists Association, 1979). New York;
The American Alpine Journal, 1981.

Williamson, Jed. and
Mobley Michael

'Editorial: "On the Razor's Edge . . ."' *The Journal
of Experiential Education*, Fall 1984.

RISK MANAGEMENT TRAINING COURSES

Weekend Courses:

Contact: NZ Mountain Safety Council
PO Box 6027
Te Aro
Wellington
Ph: (04) 385-7162

5 Day Courses:

Contact: Hillary Commission
PO Box 2251
Wellington
Ph: (04) 472-8058

FURTHER READING

(For information about accident webs and fault trees)

Davidson, G.S.

A Safety Auditing Instrument for Adventure Education, unpublished thesis, University of Minnesota, 1992.

Kates, Hohenemser & Kasperson, Eds.

Perilous Progress: Managing the Hazards of Technology, Westview Press, Boulder and London, 1985.

Snider, Wayne, ed.

Risk and Insurance. Englewood Cliffs, New Jersey: Prentice-Hall Inc., 1964.

NOTES

NOTES

RISK ANALYSIS AND MANAGEMENT SYSTEM

NAME: _____ DATE: _____

ACTIVITY/SITUATION: _____

Analysis

Description

	People	Equipment	Environment
RISKS Accident, injury other forms loss			
CAUSAL FACTORS Hazards, perils, dangers			

RELEVANT INDUSTRY STANDARDS APPLICABLE	POLICIES AND GUIDELINES RECOMMENDED